Library of
Davidson College

ON THE CORNER

ON THE CORNER
Male social life in a Paramaribo Creole neighborhood

Gary Brana-Shute
University of Utrecht, the Netherlands

Prospect Heights, Illinois

For information about this book, write or call:
    Waveland Press, Inc.
    P.O. Box 400
    Prospect Heights, Illinois 60070
    (708) 634-0081

Cover: A street scene in Paramaribo (photo by author)

Copyright © 1979 by Gary Brana-Shute
1989 reissued by Waveland Press, Inc.

ISBN 0-88133-468-5

All rights reserved. No part of this book may be reproduced, stored in a retrieval system, or transmitted in any form or by any means without permission in writing from the publisher.

Printed in the United States of America

7 6 5 4 3

Abstract

A methodological and analytical concentration on women and children biased almost all prior studies of West Indian society. A relative neglect in the study of males resulted in portraits of Afro-Caribbean society populated almost solely by women and childeren, with males depicted as "somewhat shadowy figures who drift in and out of the lives of family members" (Liebow, 1967: 5). With West Indian society described as "matrifocal" or "matricentered," matrifocality itself became an object of study without complete reference to extra-household developmental cycles, larger on-going connections with kindred, friends and neighbors, or concern with all-male groups and points of male congregation.

Behavior in all-male forums reflects and complements the social order of the communities in which men live. This manuscript deals with "men in groups": the forces pulling them together and pushing them apart; friendship and mutual aid; gossip, status and reputation building; and recruitment and expulsion. Following Chapple and Coon (1942), the drinking shop may be considered a form of association: a group of people who have established the same type of relationships with others and with each other and begin to interact regularly on that basis.

The neighborhood shop, the *winkel,* is more than a dispensary of alcoholic beverages. The *winkel* is a neighborhood waystation for lower-class men, the one neutral and accessible point in space where men with similar mating, residential and occupation arrangements can congregate and interact. These men are relatively marginal to the occupational hierarchy of "downtown" as well as to the many dispersed households and domestic groups, either consanguineal or conjugal, in which they are members. In many ways, the men who gather at the *winkel* have no place else to go.

The *winkel* as association absorbs shocks and disturbances in male interaction generated by other institutions and groups within the society. The loss of a job,

VI   *Abstract*

temporary or permanent departure from a household, the accretion or shedding of a mate, all alter a man's use of time, space, preferred activities and persons. Within the association forum a new equilibrium is established as males increase or decrease the frequency, intensity and duration of their participation with other men and, eventually, with other female-headed groups.

Gi mi boen Mati

Preface

by Alexander Moore

This book is a labor of love. It was born from the author's passionately concerned, empirically rich, and painstakingly validated two years field work in Paramaribo, Suriname. Based on a doctoral dissertation too rich to leave merely to journal articles, this book communicates the scientific findings and the human concern that motivated them. Addressed to anthropologists, their students, and educated laypersons, it is an essay in urban anthropology and an advance in Caribbean studies.

I was privileged to be Brana-Shute's doctoral advisor, and watched him come to anthropology with a dedicated interest in Caribbean and New World Black studies. He devoured the literature. As a field worker, he won rapport with Surinamers at all levels, especially with his friends of the neighborhood *winkel*, reported here. As often happens with a first-rate ethnology, the study can only do itself justice by inclusion of a large body of empirical facts. I have long advised Brana-Shute to publish a work based on his doctoral study, one in which judicious, analytic presentation of ongoing facts would flesh out the ethnological conclusions and bring them alive. This work then is intended to convey findings within carefully presented details of successful field work, the literal immersion of the ethnographer for days, weeks, and months, in the lives of his subjects.

It is this analytic but dramatic organization of the details of human action which gives the book its wide appeal to an audience not only of experts, but students and laypersons as well. Anyone interested in social structure, urban anthropology, Caribbean studies, New World Black culture, friendship and voluntary associations can further these interests here.

The study focuses — as few social science monographs do — on both the individual and the group, both the Creole neighbor and his peers at the *winkel*. Their ties are revealed as some of many personal ties in a city also portrayed, Paramaribo. The wider urban community and the neighborhood are both captured here.

Not only do we see the male side of a society usually described from the female and household point of view but we see it through the eyes of an informal association, just as the other, female, side has been described by others in the context of the household.

This book, then, is a valuable addition to the literature on voluntary associations. These have been diversely termed and are here demonstrated once again to be human shock absorbers, spontaneous neutral gathering grounds between home and work, bridges that are at once safe havens and staging grounds for a man's forays back into the public world — work — or the private world of female-dominated households.

The book then is all these social science things: treatise on urban anthropology, New World Blacks, informal voluntary associations, but it is also a human document about very human beings.

Acknowledgements

This manuscript is the final stage of my doctoral research undertaken in Paramaribo in 1972-1974. My dissertation committee at the University of Florida deserves thanks, not only for assisting me in the conception and design of the work, but also in their efforts in seeing me through its final stages. Alexander Moore Jr., my friend and doctoral supervisor, gave freely of his energy and skills in helping me bring an intelligible manuscript to fruition. Charles Wagley was always supportive and encouraged me when my laziness and pessimism prevailed. Frank Bovenkerk and Lodewijk Brunt, both of the University of Utrecht, offered their critical ethnographic comments. Frank Hughes, a former student at the University of Florida, kindly read sections of the original draft. Linda Miller of Gainesville, Florida expertly drew the diagrams contained in the dissertation and this manuscript. Rosemary Brana-Shute, apart from her own anthropological and historical investigations in Suriname, advised me every step of the way and, in the field, succeeded in situations where I would at best blunder.

I should like to thank the Foreign Area Fellowship Program and the National Science Foundation for their generous support of this research. During the write-up period I was supported by a followship from the "Man in the Tropics Program" administered through the Center for Latin American Studies, University of Florida. The Instituut voor Taal-, Land-, en Volkenkunde in Leiden kindly permitted me to reproduce portions of an article published in their journal *Bijdragen tot de Taal-, Land-, en Volkenkunde*. Mr. Hans Chin Ten Fung of Paramaribo cordially allowed me to use a piece of his photographic material for the cover.

Above all, I would like to thank the people of Suriname, especially in the neighborhood where we lived, for their unending cooperation, patience and interest in learning more about themselves and others. *Gran tangi*.

Foreword

This narrative is aimed primarily at describing certain aspects of social organization among lower-status Creole males in Paramaribo, the capital city of Suriname, South America. The term Creole in Suriname now refers to anyone accustomed to living in the coastal region who is to some degree identifiably "colored" or black. The degree of European or Afro-American cultural orientation varies considerably within this group. To be a Creole is also to suggest a town bred person or at least one who is familiar with city ways. Those Afro-Surinamers resident in rural districts, in their small villages and settlements, are called Creoles as well to distinguish them from the Maroons or tribally organized "Bush Negroes" living in the jungle interior of Suriname.

Creoles themselves recognize further distinctions within the wide and sometimes ambiguous catagory of Creole and refer to darker skinned or Negro Creoles as *Nengre*. *Nengre* also suggests a traditional culture with roots reaching back to an Afro-slave heritage. "Coloreds" are regularly referred to by the general term Creole or by the almost obsolete "Mulatto." Before the Second World War "Creole" in a restricted sense was used almost exclusively in reference to the middle class or elite "Coloreds" of European orientation while *Nengre* was applied to the Negro masses.[1] Recent opportunities for *Nengre* upward mobility have increasingly blurred these racial/cultural distinctions and lead me here to use the general term Creole throughout the following.

Even so, we cannot overlook that skin shade is still an important factor in the social organization of Suriname and that the *Nengre* possess a rich and vigorous culture that evolved in the proudest traditions of Afro-America. The influences of slavery and before — in style, expression and ideology — are identifiable. When things European — in this case Dutch — were the uncontested standards of excellence, it was the *Nengre* who jealously guarded and found comfort in their traditional culture. Many still do.

There are many other ethnic groups living in Suriname, leading many students of this society to make reference to its social and cultural pluralism. By the end of 1971, Suriname had a total population of over 385,000. Of this total were counted 118,500 Creoles, 142,300 East Indians, 58,900 Indonesians, 6,400 Chinese, 10,200 Amerindians, 4,000 Europeans, 39,500 Bush Negroes (all tribes), and 5,100 "others." Of this total population, 175,600 people, or 45.6 percent, lived in or around the capital city of Paramaribo, while 102,300 resided within the borders of the city. The distribution of the ethnic groups throughout the country varies. A breakdown of the ethnic groups resident in Paramaribo in 1965 reveals that the city contains 67,544 Creoles, 25,437 East Indians, 7,963 Indonesians, 3,869 Chinese, 2,197 Europeans, 668 Bush Negroes, and 1,741 "unknowns" (Hooghart, 1973: 10). As seen by Afro-Surinamers, Paramaribo is a Creole city surrounded by an Asian hinterland.

Migration to the Netherlands figures heavily in the demography of Suriname. Aside from sheer numbers it is reflective of a good deal more. At this moment there are approximately 130,000 Surinamers, more than one-third of the country's population, resident in the Netherlands. A yearly increase in the number of migrants was characteristic of the post-1962 period. The number of Creole migrants rose from 761 in 1964 to 4,524 per year in 1970. The East Indians registered an increase of 158 to 1,694 in the same period, while the Indonesians' increase went from 36 to 212. In evaluating these figures, Lamur points out that: "It is not surprising that the Creoles were in the majority; they are the most Westernized and the most urbanized of the three groups, and they suffer the highest rate of open unemployment" (1973: 131). Recent developments have caused these migration figures to change dramatically, causing a much larger participation of other ethnic groups in the metropolitan traffic (Bovenkerk, 1976).

Traditionally, trained positions involving higher education and specialized training have been the realm of the Creole. With the increasing integration of the East Indians and Indonesians into national society, especially through education and progressive politics, this is rapidly changing. Nonetheless, the government bureaucracy, the largest employer in Suriname, employs more Creoles than any other group and proportionally more Creoles work for the government civil service than in any other occupation.

For English-speaking students of the Caribbean Suriname has usually been a bit of an enigma. Referred to as "Dutch Guiana" (even in post-November, 1975 independence times), the country is occasionally confused with places in Africa, Asia and Indonesia. Yet, located on the northeast corner of South America, tucked between French Guiana and Brazil on the south and Guyana to the north, Suriname is very much "Caribbean" (Hoetink, 1967; Mintz, 1966 and 1974; Wagley, 1957; and van Lier, 1971) or "West Indian" (Lowenthal, 1972) if you will. Its social structure was born out of the plantation system and later social and cultural developments evolved contained and restrained by a dependency on and domination by the colonial Netherlands. Suriname's past and present have been determined and influenced by the Caribbean ecology, colonial plantation economy, introduction of African slaves and subsequent importation of indentured servants, lack of national integration and ideology and a lingering colonial ambience.

Table of contents

Abstract	v
Preface *by Alexander Moore*	vii
Acknowledgements	ix
Foreword	xi
Introduction	1
Chapter I: City and Neighborhood	6
Chapter II: On The Corner	20
A Few Characters	22
Friendship and Mutual Aid	31
Strangers, Gossip and Reputation	35
Interaction, Recruitment and Expulsion	40
Men in Groups	51
Chapter III: Off The Corner	62
Household—*Winkel* Interaction	63
A Few Tales	67
Chapter IV: Social Conflict and Ritual Restoration	81
Chapter V: Conclusion	108
Appendix	113
Notes	116
Bibliography	120

Introduction

Almost all prior anthropological studies of lower-class West Indian Creole (Afro-American) society have been biased by an analytical and methodological concentration upon women and their children. Females and children are more obvious by their regular occupation of a residential structure tied to a point in space and thus have been relatively easy to locate and identify. Personnel, usually adult males, not regularly appearing within the boundaries of four walls and a roof are overlooked or written off as "absent participants," "street corner men," and the like.

The absence or irregular participation of adult, lower-class Creole males in the household/ domestic group has been a point of methodological challenge as well as ethnographic confusion for many students of West Indian society. Conjectural, statistical, historical and sociological models have been offered in the last forty years, including the survival of Africanisms (Herskovits, 1937), the influence of European customs (Greenfield, 1966), the social organization of slavery (Frazier, 1939), ecological conditions (Steward, et al, 1956), demographic variables (Solien Gonzalez, 1969), the socio-economic status of males (R. T. Smith, 1956), the interplay of descent, alliance and inheritance patterns (Clarke, 1957), the type of mating system (M. G. Smith, 1962), and a particular colonial West Indian ideology and concern with reputation (Wilson, 1973). Still the controversy continues. In exasperation, Wilson (1973, 216) concludes that "the incredible fact is that there has been no systematic account of the social life of males and no explicit recognition, let alone analysis, of the structure and function of male peer groups."

The data on which this study is based were gathered over a two year period in Paramaribo, the capital and only city in Suriname. Although couched in a broader study of the social organization of a lower-class Creole neighborhood, I spent a good deal of time with a group of about twenty adult male Creoles ranging in age from twenty-four to sixty-two who gathered more or less regularly at a neighborhood pub (*winkel*). Apart from my interest in male bar-behavior, both as symbolic and leisure time activity, I chose to approach family and household organization by using males as my point of departure. In the early 1960's R. T. Smith suggested that we turn our attention to the networks of relationships by which various egos in particular households maintain a working system of kinship and domestic support. He stated: "the concentration ... upon the household as the functioning unit of ... organization has tended to divert attention from the networks of relationships linking households to each other" (1963:28).

With a review of the current literature on "network theory" it becomes even more obvious that we require additional description of relationships between individuals (men and women) involved in providing for households which are interconnected by links formed in exchange patterns. These interactions and strategies could best be conceptualized in processual terms. The best model could be that of R. T. Smith's (1957) developmental cycle, but applied to systems linking households and not just to the household itself.

The concentration on woman as "household head" does not illuminate all the links tying dispersed households together nor the nature and variety of male bonding to female headed groups. In the study of lower-class West Indian social organization the household as concrete unit of observation is inaccurate and misleading if the complex mating behavior, multiple residential arrangements, far flung support networks spanning many households, leisure time activities, status acquisition techniques and concepts of masculinity are to be incorporated into the discussion.

From my shop (*winkel*) vantage point I was unencumbered by omnipresent women and children engaging in obvious and expected activities in their houses and yards. Steaming pots of rice, babies bathing, spicy gossip and devilish lampoon, young girls sweeping floors and lively costumed women rushing off to market did not camouflage the relationships I was seeking. Men, when and if present, could be easily overlooked and ignored in this locus of female activity.

At the shop I could watch men come and go; leaving the household of mother, lover, consanguine or affine — it meant little difference here — and heading downtown to their jobs. If work was not available they would spend their hours at the shop and a whole other field of relationships unfolded. Nightly those employed would return to their neighborhood; neither directly nor permanently to the household, but to their sanctuary in the shop where they could gather with men who lived the same way of life.

The shop was a cross-roads for these men. It was an institution located between and articulating the worlds of downtown and the money economy and the dispersed households in which these men were members. It was from this perspective that I could best locate and identify male interactions and networks. I could see them apart from, but intimately related to, their households; at play with their peers in activities critical to their reputations and psychological well being and reacting to the capricious world of work. These male coalitions, important to the understanding of how individuals deal with kinship, household and the formal institutions of society dovetailed at the shop.

The price paid for not using an object and sample of greater breadth has been dear. The neglect in the study of males portrays whole sectors of West Indian (and Afro-American society) populated predominantly by women and children, with adult males seen as "somewhat shadowy figures who drift in and out of the lives of family members" (Liebow, 1967:5). Correspondingly, "matrifocality" in the Caribbean has often become an object of study with little reference to extra-household developmental cycles, larger ongoing connections with other levels of socio-cultural integration, or all male groups engaging in activities apart from but instrumental to the female strongholds of family, household and domestic group.[2]

The following ethnography is meant to be neither exhaustive nor contentious, but rather complementary to much of the other material produced on this topic. I choose, as mentioned, to explore the activities participated in and the nature of male interactions outside of, but critically related to, the household realm of adult women and their children.

It is appropriate to disclose some of my theoretical and methodological assumptions so that the coming data will have context and "fit," or lack of it, into prevailing notions and models. Some clues as to what started me thinking in particular directions are obvious from the sources cited in the preceeding section.

The study of "family," though concerned primarily with kinship, seemed in most cases to be undertaken by using the "household" as object and sample. Guided by this focus, the next almost inevitable step was to seize upon the adult female as "matrifocal" head of some sort of consanguineal uterine household group and begin tracing out role development and social linkages from there.

Certainly if one considers the family (kinship) or the household (residential unit) or the domestic group (cooperating, mutual maintainance coalitions) as a subsystem or subsystems related to other subsystems or social fields within society, this is a perfectly acceptable mode of procedure. However, I wanted to alter this approach and consider data from a male perspective; this led me out of the conventional anthropological world of kinship, away from house and hearth and into a social field of networks bounded by short term and not readily predictable interactions.

Networks are conceived of as having a focus, usually ego-centered, and as an individual builds up a series of personal contacts about himself, these contacts, as Mitchell has suggested (1969), vary in structure, content and meaning. It is no surprise that if we compare the networks of two different people (age, sex, status, location) we would also find that the nature of their networks varies in structure, content and meaning as well as time-table and territorial distribution. It seems unlikely that such a social reality as a unitary "total family network" comprising males and females could exist within the borders of household. The "house and yard," so very important in the Caribbean, would be misleading in this instance.

What then for the men? First needed was a reference point in space, a nexus of male aggregation and dispersal that took on regular dimensions over time. Males are certainly present in households, many men simultaneously participate in a number of them, and I could have proceeded from that location. However, I would have missed two important fields that illuminate realms of male activity in time and space and which lend texture and feeling to the culture in which men play out their lives. I needed to couple the extra-household points of male leisure time activity and recreation with a broader territorial focus in which to look at males as agents, or brokers, in exchange relationships spanning many households and interconnecting teams of women (Glaser and Strauss, 1967).

For men, as I hope some of the ethnography demonstrates, a major social and spacial focal point is the streetcorner shop or *winkel*. The men's networks, with other men and with women as consanguines and conjugals, oscillate and ebb and flow about the *winkel*. My principal chore was to identify these networks in space, the nature of linkages with other individuals and groups and the characteristics of the timetable on which they were played out. Quite apart from its function as a territorial clubhouse, the *winkel* also emerged to provide therapeutic psychological and social benefits. More of this later.

"Action-sets" (Mayer, 1966) provide me with the most dynamic appraisal of personal relationships in time and space. At any one time, any one man has created about himself a group of personnel — friends, family, intimates — constructed strategically and, perhaps, temporarily to satisfy certain needs. These relationships do not stand frozen in time but are regularly "activated, deactivated and reactivated" in the process of personal and household maintenance (Whitten, 1965). Not all the persons in ego's action-set will be in contact with each other, nor will they receive the same measure of gifts and poisons in return, nor will they maintain the same timetable and duration of participation.

Ego's action-set changes often, as personal decisions or external influences dictate. The concept also allows me to tie networks to a point in space — the *winkel* — and to articulate this male congregation point to satellite households spinning about the *winkel* each on their own time orbit. This "quasi-group," of which the action-set is the mobilized coalition of personnel contacted at any one time, is ego's working capital. These networks unfold and develop over time and exist in real, statistical terms.

The men not only inhabit a territorial unit but participate in an enduring temporal pattern of co-existences, from their births to their deaths, through roles and relationships known to their culture. Here biological time will not be concerned solely with the relentless march of the generations but rather with elements of status and role, dominance and submission, achievement and failure as men deal with one another and with women. Concepts of masculinity — its changing perception and the men's identity management — will be incorporated as well.

The *winkel* as a social shock absorber mediating disturbances in the larger system the men inhabit is a useful analogy for me. Two important social adjustments are played out in the *winkel* context: 1) the solidifying of male social relationships, and 2) actual household rearrangement as men react to changes in their domestic situations (Whitten, 1975). Following Chapple and Coon (1942, 418) the *winkel* could be considered as a form of "association": a group of people (men) who have established the same type of relationship with others (women) and with each other (as household marginals) and have begun to interact regularly on that basis. A man's *winkel* participation is in part a function of his household participation. The *winkel* as association allows men to make adjustments to disturbances in other institutions (e.g., change in household alignment, loss of a job) by allowing compensatory interaction in a neutral area along already established male lines of communication.

The places where these men spend a good deal of their time, these drinking shops that abound in Paramaribo, are not the desperate haunts of the "damned of the earth," but congregation points for males in a social organization. In a clockwork of structural time these men are reacting rationally to the process of household fission, expansion and replacement. Indeed, their streetcorner behavior demonstrates clearly that intra-household and inter-household organization itself is deeply embedded in the social system of which it is a part.

Chapter one — City and Neighborhood

> Paramaribo... has half a dozen modern buildings of which any European city might be proud. But these buildings suggesting the metropolis are incongruous in the heat and dust and afternoon stillness... for Paramaribo is provincial.
>
> (Naipaul, 1962: 183)

Fort Zeelandia lies ten miles inland on the Suriname River (Figure One). In days gone by it protected Paramaribo on the *Wilde Kust* (Wild Coast) against the incursions of the French, English, and Spanish. Until a very few years ago the post served as a civil prison, when it was renovated and converted into a national museum, each of its solid bunkers of stone block and great timbers at once housing the cultural memorabilia of each ethnic group in Suriname and separating them from each other. Artifacts retrieved from Amerindian groups deep in the bush are located on the second floor (Kloos, 1971). Drums, beads, and ritual paraphernalia and photographs attesting to past days of proud autonomy are located in the "Bush Negro" chamber at the end of the corridor (Price, 1976). The Hindustani, brought in as contract laborers in the 19th and 20th centuries, are represented here too (Speckmann, 1965). The Javanese, also imported as laborers to bolster the flagging plantation economy of post-emancipation days, find representation in this place of national symbol and sentiment through the faded photographs — photographs not so much of them as of the grounds on which they worked (de Waal Malefijt, 1963). This should come as no surprise for, as Eric Williams has said (1970), the story of the Caribbean can be told in terms of the degradation of its laborers. Looking carefully one also can find relics of the Chinese, Lebanese, Syrians, and others (de Bruijne, 1976).

The most extensive exhibits lodged in the most spacious rooms are those of the Creole and the colonial European.[3] Perhaps the two should be located in one vast chamber, for through time they have become intimately intertwined. Two groups, the African and the European, thrown together by the economic and political forces of days no one can remember, but Surinamese custom dictates they be separated.[4]

Beyond the perimeter of the officers' quarters that ring the fortress, two boulevards stretch out at right angles. Within this 90-degree arc lies Paramaribo, *foto* (downtown Paramaribo, the area behind the "fort")[5], as it is called by the native inhabitants (Figure Two).

One of these boulevards, the Gravenstraat, stretches out from the fort as far as the eye can see, to the city boundary and the Hindustani paddies beyond. Built on a mound of shells, it is the oldest street in the city. The first graveyards of Paramaribo were located along this thoroughfare. The street originates outside the fortress gates, forming the northern border of the parade grounds. Squarely in the middle of the green vastness once stood (pre-1975) a statute of Queen Wilhelmina. Today, the impressive bulk of the late Johan "Jopie" Pengel, controversial Creole Prime-minister of Suriname from 1963-1969 stands sentinel. With Independence Wilhelmina was respectfully moved, to a flower garden near the fort. Opposite and across the street sits the proud, sumptuous white mansion of the President (the ex-Governor) of Suriname. Hedges and flowers surround the driveway which runs to the foyer and past the open veranda, ending near the old palm gardens. Sentries posted at the entrance and exit usher guests and dignitaries to and from his chambers.

Almost all the formal, administrative machinery of Suriname is visible from the mansion's veranda. Ministries line the parade grounds, each with the bust of an honored civil servant before it. The parliament building, built on the foundations of the old Dutch West India Company, lies further up the Gravenstraat. Lesser sub-offices housing bureaucrats, clerks, secretaries, and milling citizens contesting water bills and sanitation services, and perhaps seeking a special favor from the very personalized Surinamese bureaucracy, spill over into the tree-lined side streets. Further on is the Roman Catholic cathedral, the second largest wooden church in the New World. Across the street is the rectory, another wooden structure. A priest in white frock and occasionally sporting a pith helmet stands on the balcony surveying the bustling city beneath him. This is possible from a third-story balcony; Paramaribo is a two and three-story city.

The Suriname Bank is next to the church. It is a modern building midst the white wooden structures with their red brick foundations, green shutters and red corrugated tin roos. The central Archives, housing material dating from the 1840's (papers from earlier days are in Holland) is here too. Until the Second World War secondary education could be sought only on this street. Miscellaneous buildings such as the water, gas, and electric utilities offices, the telephone and telegraph central, and the post office are located here abouts as well. Life can be orchestrated from the environs of "old Paramaribo." Paramaribo, with its ministry-lined central parade and streets radiating out from the fortress is unmistakably a "colonial city" (Fox, 1977). Were it not for the undulating limitations imposed by the Suriname River Paramaribo would take on a perfect gridiron pattern.

Shops, gas stations, offices, and private homes appear beyond the bank, some five hundred meters from the president's mansion. Gravenstraat is a clean, attractive street; from the sidewalk no hovels meet the eye. As with most buildings on the streetfront in the inner city, they are of wood, two-storied, with balconies overhanging the street. The people on the balconies sitting in bent wood rocking chairs behind awnings and potted plants are usually light skinned, either Dutch or colored. The black faces are on the sidewalk below. Their labors are lightened by the shade of tall cottonwood tress (*kankantrie*) that, since there was a Paramaribo, rise up from the pavement (Figure Three).

The other boulevard, the *Waterkant* (Water Side), parallels the Suriname River and in an unfaltering straight line forms the other perpendicular of the arc. This street too originates from the fort and forms the riverside boundary of the parade grounds. The Park Club, where the elite meet for dinner, drinks, and cards to discuss the future of the country and themselves, lies securely in the shadow of the old fort. A view from the seawall on the muddy riverside would show a long facade of charming two- and three-story colonial homes lining the *Waterkant* from the fortress up the street to the old pink stucco weighing house. Each building is distinctive; some with columns, some balconies, masonry stoops, great shuttered windows, and all with their red, green, and white ensembles. Paramaribo is a wooden city. These are the *herenhuizen* (gentlemen's houses), the prized high status dwellings from the days of sugar, indigo, coffee, tobacco and cotton. Although some are still private dwellings of the very rich or those with diminishing, almost residual, fortunes many have been converted to offices for companies or the government.

The houses lie close together, separated only by small alleys. A glance down one of these alleys reveals another world, a teeming arena where another style of life is played out. This is the backyard or *baka djari*. Although a geographical entity bounded by the fences of the higher born, it is an integral social building-block for the urban Creole. The back yard houses, the slave barracks and quarters of yesterday, one- and two-room cottages of grey weathered board, house the uneducated and poor. Outdoor brick ovens and wells, now decaying in disuse, sprinkle the yards that are swept clean of every blade of grass. The dry, brown turf stands in sharp contrast to the greenery of the *herenhuis*. The number of trees in the back yard is surprizing, for from the streets the city seems almost devoid of foliage. Looking skyward, the back yard sends palms and fruit trees upward. The tree is precious to these people, as life is played out in its shade and

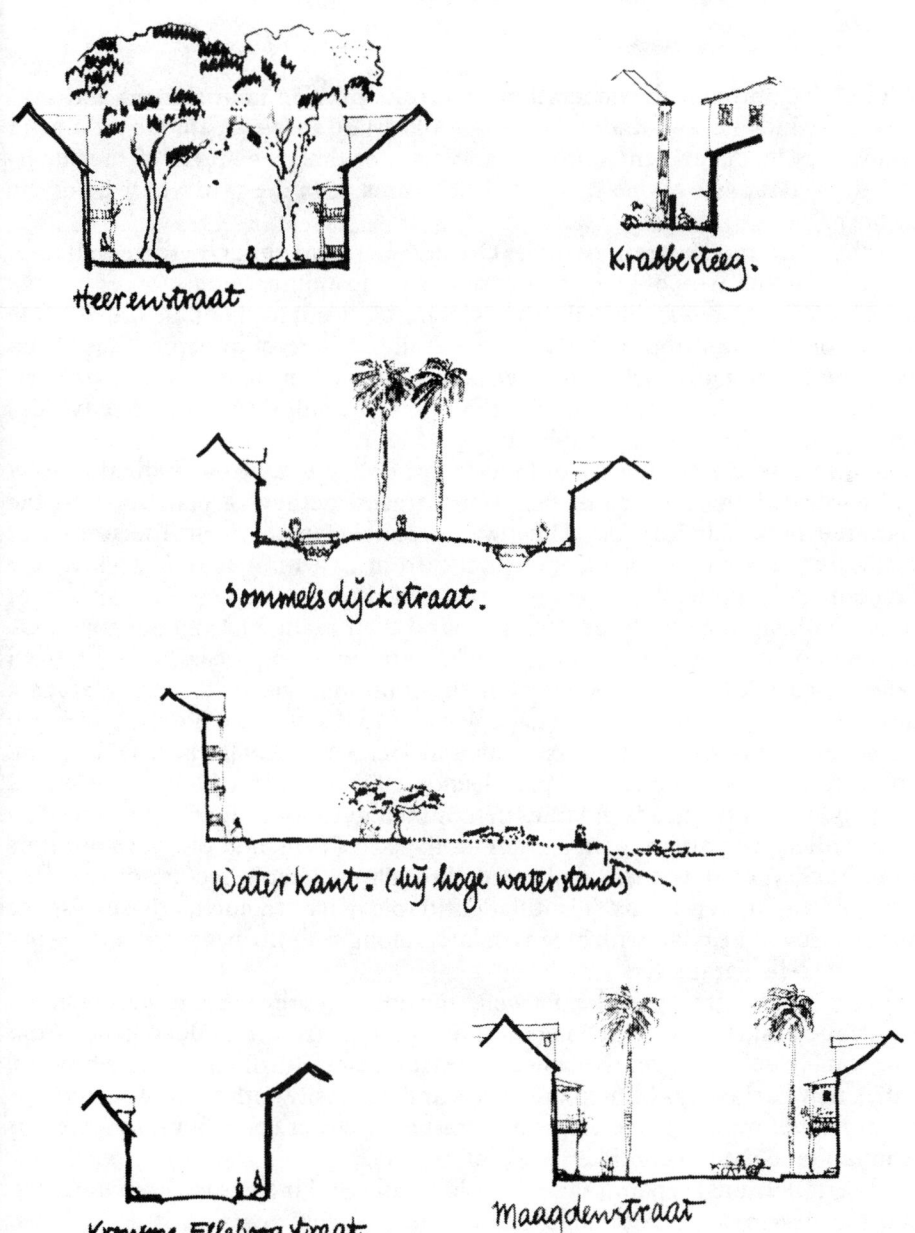

Figure three.   Paramaribo — A few typical street profiles
Source: Volders, J.L., 1966.

recapitulated through the generations, its fruits provide nourishment and supplementary income, and under the boughs of certain species roam the indulgent, mischievous or malevolent spirits of ancestors or other creatures of the supernatural. A vital piece of one's "soul" always remains in the yard where he or she was born.[6]

All the sexes and generations of the Creoles are found under these trees. Babies are cradled in the arms of their grandmothers while mothers wash clothes in large iron tubs. Young boys frolic in the dust kicking cans and tormenting lizards while girls furiously clean house attacking the endless chore of sweeping dust from inside the house out to the yard. Teenagers, dressed in their European finery, connive for a guilder or two and with their portable radios rush *foto se* (city side) to engage in the excitement of the day.

Adult men return from work or their favorite shop to take the main afternoon meal of stewed chicken or salt fish, some greens, perhaps a plantain, and the invariable mountain of rice. They will probably go to sleep afterwards, as Paramaribo shuts its doors to the public from two until four o'clock in the afternoon. All women wear something on their heads. Young girls wrap a tight fitting bandana or casually tied scarf around their plaited hair. Young women, now enamored of the Afro-fashions of North America, wear loosely woven woolen caps, while older women wear the traditional *anisa*, a stiffly starched, intricately tied head piece with each color and fold a statement on the wearer's disposition of the moment (Herskovits and Herskovits, 1936: part I). Political party affiliation was the rage in pre-election 1973 and party banners appeared wrapped around the heads of ladies determined to support their champions.

The settlement pattern, of *herenhuis* on the street front and old slave quarters in the back yard, has been replicated throughout Creole sectors of the city. Reshaped and in new forms, it is still identifiable in its structure and use of space and time. It will be dealt with at length later, along with the people who play out their lives in its parameters.

Further up the street past the old weighing house lies the harbor. It is not much by Caribbean standards. One lone dock juts into the river, to unload goods from European vessels or to receive an occasional visiting Brazilian or French patrol boat. A new harbor was built in the 1960's and lies easily within eyeshot, perhaps one and a half miles up river. This new harbor does not concern us, however, as the inhabitants do not consider it part of the city.

The ferry terminal separates the fine old houses and the harbor from the small scale business district. Suriname has in the past few years built up its road network — dirt roads are beginning to be punched through to the interior — but ferries provide the links spanning the numerous rivers. Two large ferries capable of carrying cars, trucks, motorbikes, and hordes of people and their goods ply the wide Suriname River from dawn until midnight. The traffic is endless, reaching its peak on weekends when Javanese laborers from the sugar plantations and East Indian rice farmers on the other side of the river come to town to buy. Paramaribo has been called an Afro-American city in an Asian hinterland (Buschkens, 1974). Paramaribo is largely dependent on the outside world, and Surinamers (except certain Amerindian groups) are all in some degree dependent on Paramaribo. The city's function is to provide mercantile, legal, medical, administrative, educational, communicative, and other services. Paramaribo is the only city in Suriname. Paramaribo is a dispensary.

The red-light district, located close by the old city center near Kerkplein (church square), flourishes primarily when cargo ships from Europe arrive. Business, by Caribbean standards, is slack. The rum shops and brothels in this area, and also in the seedier sections of the *Waterkant*, are peaceful and fairly safe. One leaves with the impression that these entrepreneurs are carrying on their trade in the same diligent fashion as the Chinese merchants selling medicinals, roast duck, and spices.

Beyond the ferry lies the central market. Here the tempo of life takes on a new pitch. The white shirts and ties of the bureaucrats are infrequently seen now as swarms of Creole women in gaily colored print dresses splotched with great flower blossoms, broad stripes, and bright plaids busy themselves provisioning their tables with salt meat, fish, vegetables, and rice. The roar of activity is at first deafening as bargaining, higgling, and gossiping women cluster together, their bobbing *anisas* marking the cadence of the conversation. The measured tones of Dutch are not heard here. Legs spread and strong hands akimbo on broad hips, they discuss matters of the day. These include more than the latest sexual misadventures of a common friend. Although they savor such a story and recount it with relish, they can shift swiftly to a discussion of national politics and cite from memory the personalities that play out these roles. Loud *djuries,* known elsewhere in the Caribbean as "hissing the teeth" or "jupes," punctuate the din and indicate the lip-smacker's surprise, frustrations, scorn or consternation. Paramaribo is small, and after one or two geneological citations one can easily identify at least the family of the victim under discussion. A political official, for all his pomp and dignity, finds his humanity in the market place; here he is an equal and no longer sacred. (During the past celebrations of the Queen Mother's birthday, the governor himself came to the market and danced after the market women had paraded past his house bearing flowers and singing songs.)

Reminiscences from days gone by are recalled when present members of parliament were mere children splashing naked in the gutters along the streets. Today, their occasional scandals and peccadillos are discussed with the same mirth. Many an aspiring political has foundered by not currying the favor of the Creole *moesjae* (respected older woman). Lampoon and ridicule deftly wielded today as yesterday (when it was an important weapon wielded by the slaves) has set many a Holland-educated hopeful to running.

Familiarity may breed contempt but it also fosters a consistent attitude to overlook fault and foible if the guilty party behaves with respect and good manners. A sort of "provincial morality" (Gans, 1962) is at work here. Less than ethical behavior may well be written off as boldness, precociousness, or self-interest; traits shared, or at least appreciated, by many.

The market, today with a more East Indian complexion than Creole, is a large concrete and iron quonset hut on the site of the old, open riverside market. The bottom floor is laden with tropical fruits and vegetables of all types. Creoles sell most of the ground crops (cassava, peanuts, yams, etc.); East Indians and Javanese the fruits and leafy greens. Upstairs, imported foods (potatoes and onions), spices, canned goods and dry goods, are sold. Specialists selling ritual paraphernalia and obeahs sit confidently at stalls beside basket makers and women dispensing fruit drinks.

Behind the main market are more vegetable stands and the fish and poultry market. Creole women still seem to monopolize the fish trade as they hawk crab and other manner of fish. Many of these women fish themselves or are supplied by family members. Open canoes and tent-boats, now with outboard motors, unload their wares every morning at sunrise. Here is a repository of tradition and lore found nowhere else in Paramaribo. To confirm a story, a piece of hearsay, or learn the preparation of a supernatural potion, one comes to *baka wowoyjo* (behind the market) and seeks out a trusted elder. Surinamers are careful here; careful because of their fear of strangers and also of young boys who steal purses and carefully concealed caches of money which women hide in knotted handkerchieves under their brassieres. One is always cautious and casts an eye on all passersby. The stranger is mistrusted; a glance that lingers can mean only trouble. "They" seek your money through swindle, false friendship, or theft; or worse, they seek to learn your fancies and weaknesses and through this knowledge manufacture a charm to control or exploit you and yours.

The market provisions Paramaribo and its suburbs and so sets a tempo for the flow of human traffic in and out of the city. Busses line the streets, each to cart off a load of people and their goods to a different neighborhood. These "wild"

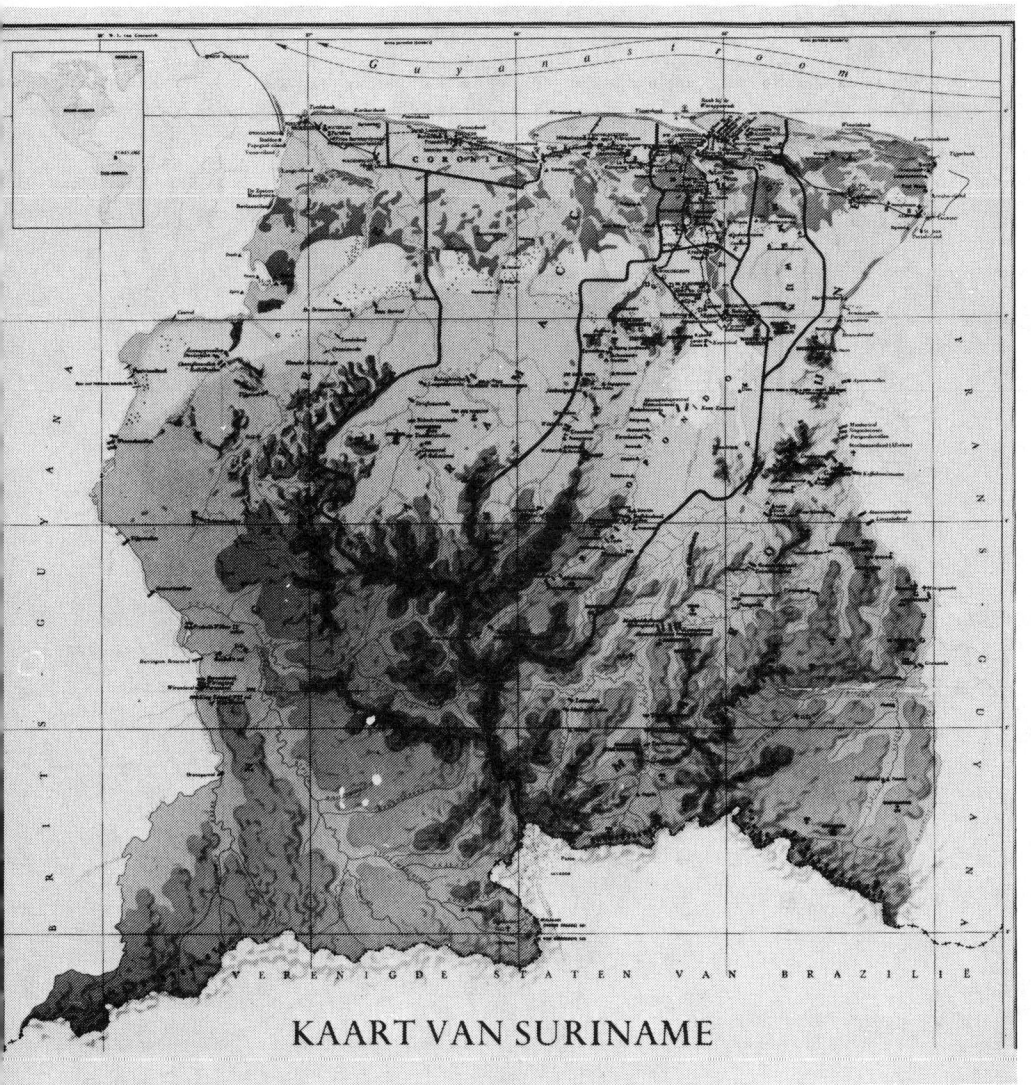

Figure one. Map of Suriname
Source: Dahlberg, H. N. n.d.

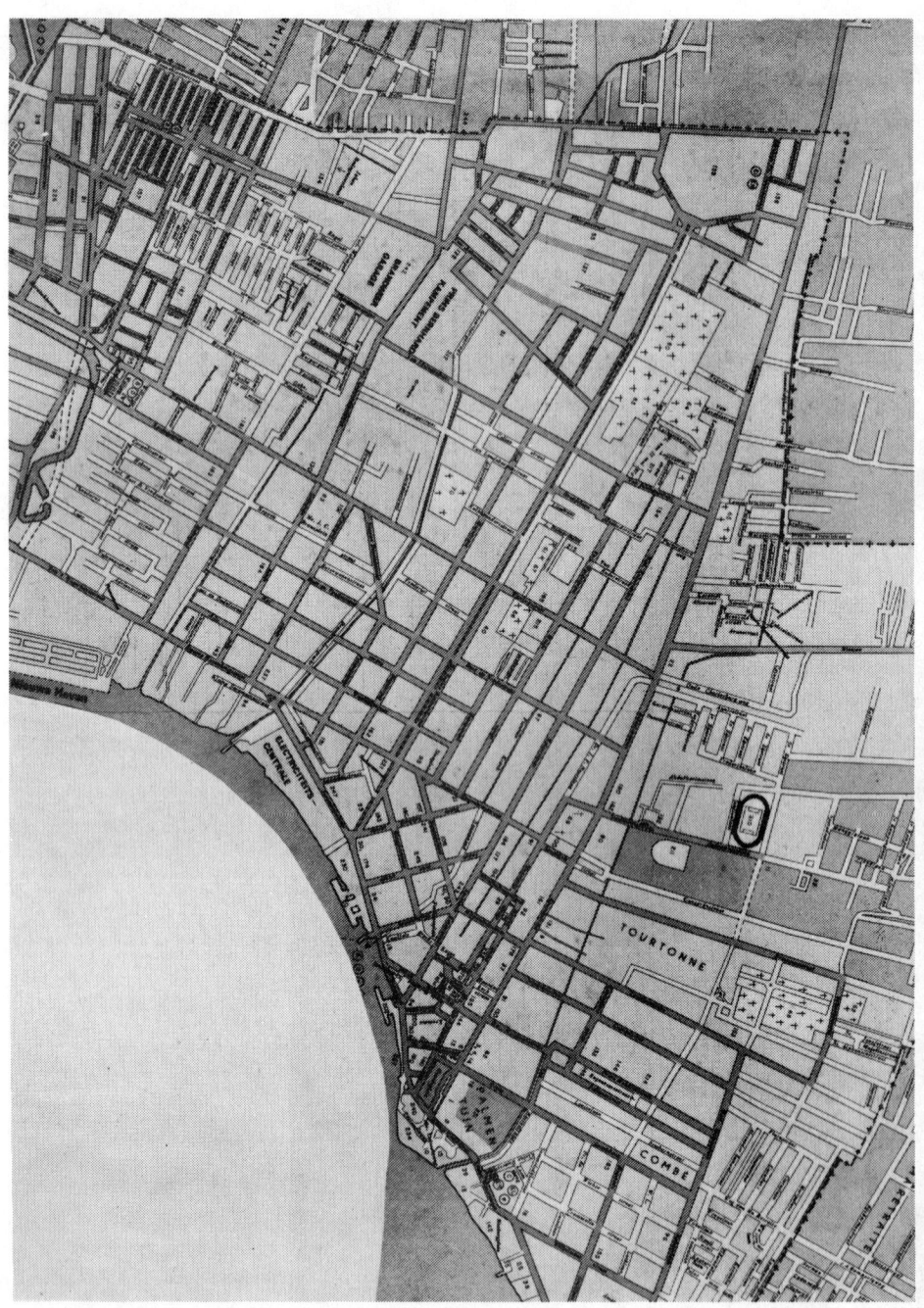

Figure two. Map of Paramaribo
Source: Vaco, n.d.

busses, usually a VW bus with a fifteen person capacity that is always exceeded, are owned principally by East Indians, a fact causing some indignation for the Creoles virtually dependent on them.

The Waterkant intersects two other avenues and continues on its way, now renamed the Saramaccastraat after the Saramaka Bush Negroes who used to reside in its lodges and flophouses during their periodic trips to town in the old days. The buildings take on a dingy cast, although they are still the wooden structures of downtown. Anything can be bought on Saramaccastraat. The Chinese and Lebanese merchants see to that. Store fronts overflow into the street with bins of corks, cloth, rope, lanterns, machetes, shovels, candies, hammocks, and electric appliances. The small shops that line the Saramaccastraat and appear everywhere else in downtown Paramaribo service not only the material but the physical as well. Men cluster here and drink beer, rum, and whiskey at makeshift wooden bars in the corner midst dusty buckets, lines of hemp, and bicycle tires hung from the ceiling. Women returning from the market, the shoe stores, and clothiers stop in for a beer or soft drink and bread. Women are not excluded from these *winkel* bars, but they play a very restricted role in order to avoid trouble and embarrassment.

In the *winkel* languages are a babel. Clusters of Bush Negroes speak their tribal languages while an occasional Amerindian calls out to his wife walking a few paces behind. Chinese voices count the day's profits on their abacuses, midst the Hindustani and Javanese that punctuate the din. Creoles talk amongst themselves in city *Sranan Tongo*. Conversations across ethnic boundaries take place in this language as well. Meanwhile, Dutch pours from the radio and peers up from the crumpled newspapers on the floor.

The Saramaccastraat continues on in such a fashion for another 500 meters. Restaurants, more for take-out food than sit-down meals, are situated among the drinking bars and sundry shops. Many of the *winkels* would be in poor financial straits were it not for the sale of liquor to men.

Behind the facade of the *winkels* and buildings on the riverside of the street lies the waterfront proper. Shipyards, drydocks, repair shops, construction companies, carpentry shops, heavy machine storage, timber depots and the like line the river bank. Open gutters spilling refuse into the river mingle trash with the oil and machine residue. The muddy ground gives way underfoot. The stench and by-products of everything mechanical fortunately do not spill over onto the Saramaccastraat which remains surprisingly clean and well kept for such a heavily trafficked artery.

Until the 1950's a railroad from the gold and rubber (*balata*) fields deep in the interior ran into Paramaribo along this main street. Today the line exists only in diminished form, its jungle end shortened by an artifical lake formed by a hydro-electric dam built in the 1960's to provide energy for aluminum processing and its city-side trunk cut short thirty kilometers outside the city in the village of Onverwacht. The ubiquitous motor scooter and mini-bus fill the transportation vacuum. People remember the days when the old steam engine would chug into town along the hardpacked dirt streets. Up past the central market it would go, by crowds of women and children waving on the street corners, to deposit the men all laden with new wealth on the Heiligeweg near the ferry. Today, this once happy depot is the terminal for the government bus lines. Nor are there open gutters anymore that once lined the streets and were traversed via an outstretched plank. The downtown streets are paved too. All this since the late 1950's.

The terminus of Saramaccastraat is a stone bridge that spans the Drambrandersgracht (-*gracht* is a canal or drainage ditch). Beyond this point lives the bulk of the Creole population in urban neighborhoods. Over the bridge the pace of life is slower, taking on an almost rural cast within the formal city borders of Paramaribo.

Downtown Paramaribo, the inner city, stops at Drambrandersgracht. The people who live behind the Drambrandersgracht call it *foto se* (city side), although most Creoles could never arrive at a mutual accord as to exactly where *foto se* begins or ends. Until emancipation most Creole slaves lived either on the plantations along the rivers or in this downtown area of the city where they toiled as domestic slaves. A very important portion of the pre-emancipation Creole population did not live downtown. They were the free people of color and resided over the Drambrandersgracht in an urban neighborhood called *Frimangron* (Free Man's Ground). That area, now engulfed, but not dissolved, by metropolitan Paramaribo, is known by that same name to this very day.

Today the downtown area houses almost all the service and distributive agencies in Suriname. Large companies such as Bruynzeel (wood processors and exporters), the Surinam-American Aluminum Company, the Wageningen rice cooperative, and the "Industrial Park," are located outside of Paramaribo; but these are all recent innovations, overlays that came in the immediate past. Virtually everything else is located within the broad arc bounded by the two boulevards; government offices, secondary schools (for most of the country), the university (for medicine, law, and recently social studies), banks, foreign embassies, restaurants, shops, tailors, department stores, butchers, book stores, pharmacies, labor union halls, churches, political party headquarters, courts, police stations, lawyers' offices, newspaper publishers. All the formal organs necessary to organize and maintain a nation state are here.

Creoles like Paramaribo. Although most comfortable in the security and friendship of their own neighborhood (*birti*), they enjoy downtown. Certain places invoke living memories of days gone by. And now, the story of a car accident on this corner, a ship sunk there, a woman possessed by a certain spirit under that tree, a bridge guarded by night by certain supernatural creatures is passed on in a rich and expressive oral tradition. A mythology has grown up around most parts and buildings of the city, that ties sentiment to points in space. Before the Second World War, citizens would often commemorate an event with a specially created proverb or poem and special *anisa* (Herskovits and Herskovits, 1936: part I).

Street names have been informally changed from the cumbersome Dutch to the more manageable and meaningful *Sranan Tongo*. The unwieldy Dokter Sophie Redmondstraat became *ondro bom* (under the tree, for the large trees that once lined the avenue); likewise Pad van Wanica (the Wanica road) is also Para *passie* (the footpass to the District Para). The personalization of Paramaribo stretched even into the *baka djari*. A known occurrence or sorcerer, or perhaps just somebody with a unique characteristic drew forth a reference that everybody could identify. *Popki-djari* (yard of the dolls), *Para-djari* (Para yard), *froitiman-djari* (whistling man yard), *lanti-djari* (government yard), and others elicited considerably more enthusiasm than the austere formality of the Dutch appellations. For many Creoles things are known by personal experience. Street corners and special areas carried not the name Ladesmastraat, but rather *tingi-oekoe* (stinky corner) and *winti-oekoe* (wind or spirit corner). The corner of Gemenelandsweg and Zwartenhovenbrugstraat became *spoendoro,* referring back to the days when the old steam engine bringing back the miners would make its first city stop at this spot.

If certain places are loved then certain places are feared. The *amandra* (almond) trees lining the Waterkant must be avoided at 12 noon and 11 o'clock at night for it is then that the *bakroe* (short manlike, malevolent creatures, half wood and half flesh) lurk beneath them. And the church on the Wanicastraat should be avoided at night, as years ago an unsolved murder took place there, and most people will tell you the suspect was not human.

Drainage ditches and gutters cross-cut Paramaribo. Once they drained the plantation flat lands surrounding the city. Now most of the broad gutters are filled and covered, some converted into attractive, tree-lined malls. Others still carry filth in open ditches through the city to the river. These gutters and ditches serve as boundaries with some residential areas today carrying the name of the gutter that runs close by it. Before World War II and their subsequent filling in, these networks of water control were spanned by arched stone bridges, and the passage to the other side of the arch was a clear statement that another area of the city was being entered.

The Drambrandersgracht is one of these ditches. It is filled in except for a short piece beginning about 150 meters from the river bank. An old sluice gate with great pulleys and sliding iron doors stands sentinel on the sludge that frequently accumulates.

Drambrandersgracht is a very real border; officialdom considers it one of the boundaries of *wijk F* (a neighborhood division used at the Bureau of Deeds and Records) and so notes it in all the great books of the state. Political parties know the people beyond Drambrandersgracht share a common tradition and sentiment and have located two or three party cells there for recruitment and propaganda purposes (Brana-Shute, R., 1976). The folk, however, know best of all what it means to live behind Drambrandersgracht. It means to live in an almost rural neighborhood where sentiments and social relationships forged though not frozen under slavery — and before — still flourish in many forms. Above all, it means to live in the place most Creoles know as *Frimangron*.

Over the years *Frimangron* has changed. Up until the 1950's the main streets of the area were little more than one-lane dirt paths. Lining each side of the street, between it and the houses, were open drainage ditches and gutters overgrown with trees and bushes. Mostly people chose to walk in the open road, for although there were cleared paths through the bush along the gutters these were the feared *Yorka* (ancestral ghosts) paths, where ghosts and evil creatures (and thieves!) lingered in wait for their mortal victims. Electricity and running water came to Paramaribo late in the 1920's, but did not arrive in *Frimangron* until much later. Even today asphalt does not cover every street, nor water and electricity penetrate every back yard. Back yard barracks and cottages, some about to collapse from the weight of age, still house most of the people living in *Frimangron*.

Almost all the houses on the street front are made of weathered wooden plank aged to a light grey. They are either two story or one story with a tiny attic. Houses in the back yards are not nearly so nice; many have only one wee room and a cooking area (Figure Four).

A *winkel* stands on every corner of *Frimangron*. Most are owned by Chinese some by Hindustani, none by Creoles. The rest of the street is taken up by private homes, tailor shops, repair shops, fish and fruit vendors, take-out restaurants elementary schools, a Catholic or a Moravian church, and other small scale

City and Neighborhood 17

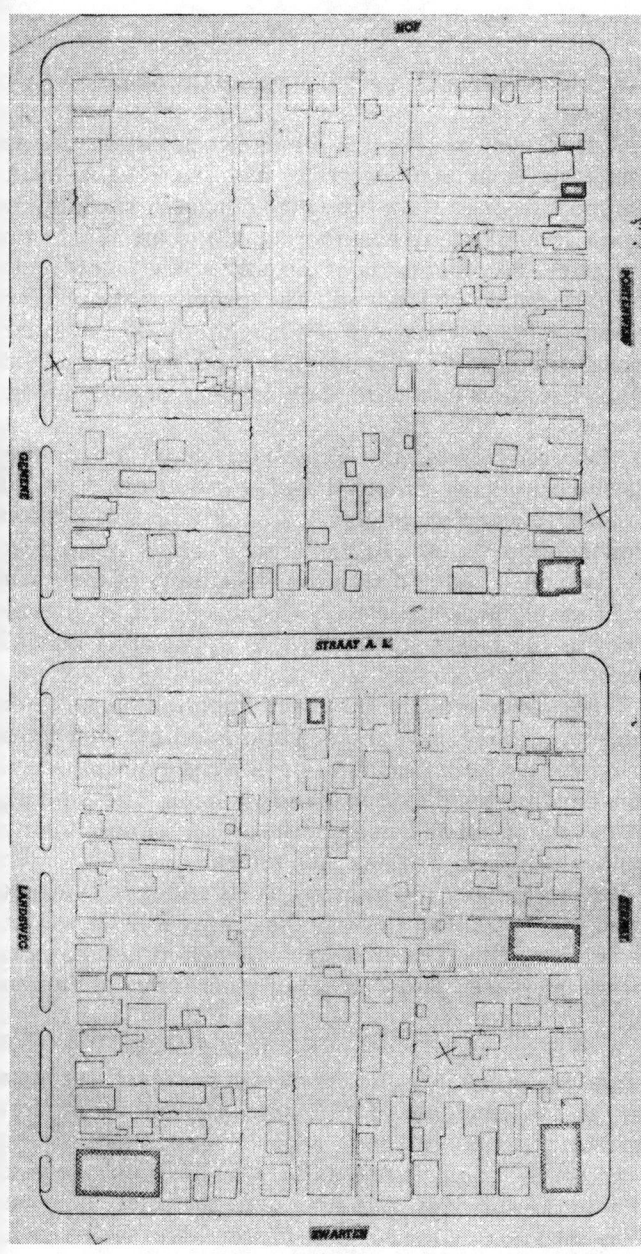

Figure four. Partial map of Neighborhood F - Frimangron
Source: Centraal Bureau Luchtkartering, 1965.

businesses. All these shops are small, privately owned, and usually operated on a part-time basis (except the *winkels*).

Frimangron is closely tied into downtown Paramaribo. Police patrol the streets and offenders and lawbreakers from murderers to men who have been delinquent in their child support payments are brought to the courts. Children attend the elementary schools located in the neighborhood, and are taught by teachers from other social classes and other parts of the city. A few follow their education through to the universities in Holland. The people make use of hospitals, clinics, and government welfare services. If a neighborhood extension of these national institutions is not located in the neighborhood, the main office is but ten minutes away by bus. Endless lines form daily in front of government offices downtown on the square.

Resident Catholic, Jehovah's Witnesses, and Protestant clergy are in the neighborhood and along with supplying financial and spiritual aid baptize, marry, confirm, and bury the people of *Frimangron*.

Women, in their occasional shopping tours in the larger stores of downtown and daily at the central market, must contend with the vissicitudes of the open market system. Money spent at the market is usually disbursed to East Indian vendors, while money spent in the larger stores flows to upper class Dutch, Lebanese, or Portuguese merchants who control large scale retailing.

The men who live in *Frimangron* provide the most important links with downtown. Everyday, if employed, they leave the neighborhood for their jobs. Unless self-employed, as a carpenter, auto mechanic, or flowerpot maker — few are — all men must leave the neighborhood to seek their livelihood. The women, children, and small scale merchants of the neighborhood are almost totally dependent on the wages with which these working men return.

Frimangron is closely linked to Paramaribo at many levels and is in constant adaptation to the fluctuations of larger society. For all the connections, however, there are boundary maintaining mechanisms that set the neighborhood apart; different behavior patterns taking place in the context of other forms of human groupings.

About 6,800 people live here (Algemeen Bureau voor de Statistiek, 1973: 16)[7] and although their social connections stretch into downtown they play out their lives in *Frimangron*. Most of the residents of *Frimangron*, even by modest government guidelines, are financially poor. Some, particularly aggressive young men enjoying Suriname's industrial "boom," are not. Just who has money, where they get it, what they do with it, who they give it to, and the effect of these variables on the table of organization of the neighborhood, is the sociological point of departure for the following chapters. The *winkel* is the focus of our attention here. Its function as a dispensary of necessities and as a meeting place structures much of the rhythm of daily and weekly time, and later influences the arrangements a man may make with kith and kin as he passes along the life cycle.

Chapter two — On the corner

> Te joe lobi wan oema, joe moe' loek' en gogo. If a baka lolo, joe moe' djar' censi. (When you like a woman, you must look at her buttocks. If her backside shakes from side-to-side, you must bring money.)
> (The Twinklestars: 1974)

In *Frimangron,* as in low income communities elsewhere in the Caribbean, the streets are divided, or set apart by specific locations, typically corners where boys and men congregate at certain times during the day and evening hours to "lime."[8] At most of these locations, and certainly the key ones, there is a *winkel,* which provides a background setting for the collective activities taking place.

For male and female, young and old, all day and into the evening hours, the *winkel* is a major point of neighborhood aggregation and dispersal. They come to buy rice, oil, spices, canned goods, butter, batteries, bouillon cubes, combs, perfume, toys, tea cups, ice, Chinese medicinals, fire crackers, and alcohol. One does not buy all the day's goods at one time; one or two items are always left wanting so that a person may have an excuse for returning and looking in on this entertaining and important arena.

It is the alcohol that ostensibly attracts the men. At any time from seven in the morning to ten o'clock at night, groups of men of varying dress, deportment and skin shade congregate here to drink whiskey, rum, beer and cognac. They sit at tables or lean on the glass cases; perhaps the *winkel* might even sport a small, sit-down bar. Women and children continually dart in and out, sometimes having a word with the neighborhood men who are, for the first time, localized after their separate journies and experiences.

Women do not linger here; their respectability is at stake. Men, however, linger, and midst the story telling, drinking, fraternity, and disbursement of great quantities of money the realities of kinship, residence, mating, friendship and domesticity mesh.

The *winkel* is in many ways a bridge; a waystation between the men's world of commercial downtown Paramaribo and the women's world of the household and neighborhood. It is downtown where the male fulfills his major social role (or has it crushed) in the occupational hierarchy of business and government. Regularly or erratically when employed he interacts with and in this hierarchy for his wages, the resources upon which household-heading females are critically dependent. Evening, leisure time and unemployment find the male back in the neighborhood spending most of his time in the *winkel* rather than the household. The dynamics of adult male social organization, the roles he is expected to play out, are almost centrifugal, spinning men out of the household and neighborhood and into the realm of salaries and wages.

Women form their most resilient and intense ties with other females in the neighborhood, within kin-based households, and with friends, neighbors, and club members. The dynamics of adult female social organization are rather centripetal; relationships devolve in upon the household and upon other households in the neighborhood. Social clubs, burial associations, rotating credit organizations and, even, political party cells, are prominent female activities. Women invest and consolidate their social capital in confines that do not regularly penetrate the formal occupational structures of downtown.

However, males and females are interdependent, and neither can exist without at least the partial services of the other. They do, at various times, link up. Their worlds articulate as though spinning on two separate axes. The most frequent meshing point is the *winkel*. Adult males are present in households; they regularly sleep, eat, have sex, and have other services performed for them there. They visit women in their houses and yards, or, more cautiously, occasionally meet them on the corner or through the *winkel's* open window, to provide them with money for services rendered, promised or anticipated, for child support payments or just because the fellow was in a jolly or flamboyant mood. However, if one looks at the world of men, and the dynamics of social organization above the household level – a sort of bird's eye view of the neighborhood over time – the spatial nexus of male-female interaction is not the household but rather the local *winkel*; the neighborhood cross roads of city and household.

The *winkel* is an easily penetrated male sanctuary. For whatever purposes, women can locate and negotiate with men in this sedentary point. A woman abused – usually a neglected girlfriend – can deal a mighty verbal blow to her man hob-nobbing with the fellows. Scorn, heaped on in public, for taking the very food from her mouth by withholding precious guilders; or perhaps, more accurately, by putting food in another undeserving female mouth, is an excoriation most males prefer to do without during their leisure *winkel* hours.

Men not only form temporary and semi-permanent alliances with other men, but also with clusters of women, conjugal and consanguineal, dispersed in different households. If a man is shrewd these households will not be located in the same locale. Many times however, this is unavoidable. At any time any one of these men from his *winkel* headquarters has activated a series of relationships with women. Some contacts are terminated, some activated, others reactivated, many overlap. Males do not regularly establish only one household relationship at a time, and as a result have the same commitments to many females simultaneously. Their resources must be given wisely as they are instrumental to the survival of a number of groups of women. It is a sorry day — and cause for great glee for the on-lookers — when two or more women sharing the same man arrive on the corner. More of this later.

A) *A Few Characters*

In the center of one of the largest inner-city lower-class Creole neighborhoods of Paramaribo stands the *winkel* of Chung the Chinese. This is a very special *winkel*. It is clean and spacious, and the owner is not above friendly banter with the Creoles on whom his business rests and to whom he extends credit. Well located it has a reputation as a friendly, safe, and enjoyable place to congregate. Most importantly for the male patrons, largely residents in and around the neighborhood, it enjoys a license that permits the sale of all hard liquors. This corner is also auspiciously placed, a location where one can observe the traffic of the day. Male passersby from other city sections regularly drop in during their work rounds for a beer or soft drink and enliven any conversations underway with news of other people, places and goings-on. When things do quiet down the men watch the world go by, and in their quiet, invest the most mundane of things with an active, though spurious, glamour.

At seven o'clock in the morning the heavy green shutters of the *winkel* are still boarded shut. Undeterred, a customer who pushes open the tall doors will find a fleshy Chinese sweeping away the residue of last night's gathering. Chung speaks little Dutch, but his regular customers find this no trouble as they prefer his *Sranan Tongo* anyway.

For Sf 3.50[9] one can order a half pint of American whiskey and get with it a glass, bottle of cold water, and a small bowl of ice cubes from Chung's freezer. A customer could have chosen from a wide stock of local and imported beers, domestic and foreign rum, Dutch gin, brandy, or any one of the many brands of whiskey offered. Like many of the Creoles who come here, most drink whiskey and look down their nose at the local rums which they feel are inferior to American products. Although much cheaper, rum is infrequently drunk. The excuses offered; upsetting digestion, wretched hangovers, instant intoxication and loss of memory are not above suspicion. A whiskey drinker is a well situated man, or so everyone likes to think.

Although the personnel who congregate at any one time varies, the daily time-table is fairly routine. Arrival commences early in the day for those with a day off, unemployed or awaiting a later shift. After rising at five-thirty or six o'clock and taking a breakfast of tea and bread, an adult male, residing with either blood kin or affines, repairs to his chores in the house and yard. Knocking fruit from trees, mending the chicken koop or carrying back to the house a heavy cooking-gas bomb are usual fare. By nine o'clock, should nothing else be wanting, it can be safely assumed that a man will look into the *winkel*.

Across the street from the *winkel*, a man in his fifties opens the alley gate to a grey, weathered cottage and rolls his bicycle out onto the street. He wears battered rubber sandals on his feet, differentiating him from most of the other people hereabouts who prefer the dignity of shoes. His wrinkled pants are cinched around his great paunch with a piece of rope; a white shirt is stuffed willynilly into his trousers. Around his neck he wears a slender gold chain, the only item lending elegance to his demeanor. The color of his skin is black and he is obviously not at all well to do. Entering the *winkel*, he walks to the counter and, before ordering, greets those present with a collective "good morning *mijne heren*." Today he must drink beer, it is towards the end of the month and his funds are low.

This is Russel (as he is known to everyone) and he lives with Betty. Today he is in the *winkel* in the morning, as his job as custodian at an office downtown rotates him on shifts. Next week he will come to the *winkel* in the afternoons and the week after that in the evenings. Today Russel will stay here until 1 o'clock when he goes home for lunch. If it is not prepared and laid out on the table for him there will be trouble. To Russel it would suggest that he is being snubbed, or worse, that his woman has no respect for the "working man." With only a tenuous hold in Betty's house, he tries to demand respect — at least.

From Russel's Sf 215[10] monthly salary he gives Sf 10 piece to the mothers of the two children he fathered through visiting relationships and Sf 57 to Betty. The remainder of his salary, except for an occasional item such as a radio, is spent at the *winkel* and on gifts for women he is currently visiting. He has openly engaged in a number of affairs and people in the neighborhood funneled the word back to Betty. A few days ago he bought an expensive bottle of perfume for one of his lady friends and announced to all assembled in the *winkel* that he was going to her at that moment. When Betty heard this she remarked that he does not even bring her a can of beer.

Among the men who gather regularly at the *winkel*, Russel has a poor reputation and is often the object of crude jokes. Consensus has it that he is sloppy and dirty (*morsoe*; a particularly strong indictment from a people who are very concerned about body cleanliness). He is also a gossip, a not to be trusted loudmouth. Everyone gossips, but judiciously, with desired ends in mind, with certain people, and at proper times and places. Gossip in many ways functions as a recruitment mechanism and boundary maintaining device in the formation of groups. If one is privy to gossip from a certain group one responds in kind, and one participates with few other groups. To do so would compromise credibility in the original group and threaten its internal equilibrium by signaling out certain of its members as potential targets for harmful gossip that the gossiper intentionally or inadvertently passed on. Russel is gossiped about, and he gossips to many people, but only rarely is he gossiped "with."

Two men approach the *winkel* from different directions. One of them arrives by car and is smartly dressed. He used to come regularly every morning at 10 o'clock from his post in business and stay for one drink or many depending on how urgent the day's work was. Since getting embroiled in a controversial issue that conflicted with the execution of his work he left the job to do piece-work for a local newspaper. This is Schill, a friendly, intelligent man in his fifties, a principal character in the *winkel*.

Marcell, on the other hand, approaches by foot. He is a dark-skinned man in his early twenties, dressed very casually in modish slacks and a pull-over jersey. He saunters with a slightly arrogant air and gives the impression he is one of the "choke and rob" boys that victimize people in poorer sections of Paramaribo. However, he is not. Rather he holds a position as a highly skilled blue collar worker and with overtime pay draws one of the highest salaries in the neighborhood. With his money he, like all the other men in the *winkel*, supports a number of households containing kin and friends.

The unlikely pair meet, sit down together at the same table with the others and share a bottle of whiskey. Marcell calls to the barkeep to put it on the credit tab he pays every fortnight.

When Schill talks people in the *winkel* listen. By neighborhood standards he is a man of streetcorner letters and knows, or at least is acquainted with, people in higher places. Schill presides over these forum-like dialogues in the *winkel* and his opinion is held in high esteem by the men. It seems to be only the women, watching and listening to Schill preside, who ask the question "if you are so important what are you doing here?"

Although Schill is not entirely what he says he is, he does have connections, and at times acts as a broker between persons — men and women — in the neighborhood and certain well placed patrons in business and government. It is a rare white collar bureaucrat that ventures into the lower-status residential areas of Paramaribo. Every neighborhood has a "Schill" and these brokers all act in roughly the same fashion by establishing personal contact with higher status neighborhood personages, being on good terms with the older teenagers, dispensing favors — sometimes mere trifles — and passing information up and down. If these brokers are shrewd — and Schill is — they will establish cordial relationships with neighborhood women who, in their social clubs and political party cells, are involved in numerous overlapping activities and relationships that integrate clusters of women within the neighborhood. Such female coalitions are mobilized regularly for good fun and mutual aid as well as the quite serious business of propagandizing and mobilizing the vote during election times (Brana-Shute, R., 1976). Men, by contrast, are dispersed far and wide tending to their work and multiple household responsibilities. Rarely do they form corporate neighborhood common interest groups.

His roving eye led to Shill's dismissal by his last woman and, to fill the vacuum, he began to spend more and more time at the *winkel*. He still has his laundry done by her, a service for which he pays, but eats at his sister's and visits other women for sexual purposes. Elaborating his ties in the neighborhood he became close to the women's political party cell (*kern*) and provided them with advice on organization and how to deal with the formal power structure staffed by the technocrats. His contacts with people were personal and "many stranded" and soon Schill became a familiar part of the area. He could be counted on to provide a few guilders for a needy mother, to arrange (*regelen*) a job, as perhaps street cleaner or watchman, and to tend to small scale matters necessary for the daily existence of the people. Useful to the neighborhood and higher-ups alike, he is satisfied with respect from the former and an occasional piece of the action from the latter.

While others listen to Schill's deliveries, Marcell stares out the window, his eye seizing upon every moving object. Last night he worked the night shift outside the city and rode on the dusty, guttered dirt road the 20 kilometers back to Paramaribo to enjoy his day off before returning again that afternoon. The saw-mill that employs him provides food and shelter for the men who work there but, without the excitement of Paramaribo, many men do not like it and prefer the long daily journey back to *foto* (city). He arrived in Paramaribo at 2 o'clock in the morning, slept until 9 o'clock, drank a glass of ice water and came to the *winkel*.

At this point Marcell is enjoying the favors of five women, including the one he is currently living with; he has the economic resources to do it. When the women are short of money they can come to him for aid; his periodic disbursals of anything from small change to upwards of Sf 100 make him invaluable. They all know where to find him and often in the evenings a whisper through the *winkel* window will draw him outside. He may call upon them for services (sex, running an errand, housecleaning) that evening, the next day, or next week. The connection may remain latent often reactivated first by a woman.

During the last monthly pay period Marcell worked overtime and brought home Sf 435.[11] This is a high salary and by national financial standards would place Marcell solidly in the middle income range. However, Marcell is in debt to the company bank and his paternal aunt, and at the end of every pay period he is penniless.

He has Sf 25 left from the Sf 435 check he received a little over a week ago. The money found its way to many people. Chung, the *winkel* proprietor, got Sf 102 for Marcell's two week alcohol bill. (Some women support themselves and their children on less than Sf 60 per month.) Sf 100 went to the woman with whom he is now living. She uses the money to buy clothes, food, jewelry, household decorations and appliances (for their two room, worn cottage), and to make contributions to her family who are poor. Because he lived with his paternal aunt off and on for the last 11 years, Marcell gave her Sf 50. To care for her children he gave the aunt's daughter, his cousin, Sf 30. Sf 25 went to Silvia a woman with whom he occasionally visits, as well as Sf 10 for another of his girl friends. The other three young women he visits got nothing this paycheck. His sister looked him up at the *winkel* yesterday and he gave her Sf 10. House rent at Sf 14 and utilities completed his disbursals.

Asked if he would consider banking portions of his salary, Marcell scoffs at the idea. Much better, he reasons, to be a man of means, indulging pleasures and investing money in persons and possessions, both of which, incidentally, can be converted into cash when need be. Money serves no apparent use in the bank, especially when you need it in a hurry.[12] His women and his friends are many, and a number of people in the neighborhood are beholden to him — for a loan, a gift to an old penniless woman, a bicycle bestowed on a young child. Marcell has a big heart. Besides, he continues, he chooses not to be with just one woman, and through his disbursements has a number at his disposal. One of them, he presumes, will always forsake you in a pinch so better to increase the odds in your favor. He is also admired by the men for his rather spectacular social and sexual feats. Even when his relationships went sour across the board (see Chapter IV) his dilemma provided daily entertainment and food for conversation for the entire neighborhood.

For Marcell, and many of the men, money has a profound meaning and often becomes an existential part of "self." On it depends a good deal of Marcell's identity; the life style, ambience and confidence with which he conducts himself on the streets. Downtown, with those of loftier status in the national society, his bankroll would be superceded by other qualities — skin shade, lack of formal education and grooming, his "tough-guy" demeanor — to which all are attached a negative valence. But here, in the neighborhood, money and all its extensions fixes him within the circle of *winkel* friends, kin and paramours as a man of enviable life style. Pleasures can be purchased and "sweet talk" supported with evidence of tangible favors. Marcell's fortune, maintaining and ensuring contacts, gives him a profound self-awareness that enhances his presentation in everyday neighborhood encounter. Here he is no fake, no bogus hustler in a fantasy world of his own creation, but one, who if in a position or commitment that has to be shored up with a new pair of shoes or a liter of rum, then so be it. His money, though carefully monitored, is public.

Marcell will stay at the *winkel* until about two o'clock today. He will eat later with Sissy, his paternal aunt, because the woman with whom he lives is away. There is no set eating hour. A pot of rice with vegetables and fish is always on the stove and Marcell needs only take a portion and retire to a meal under the trees in the back yard. If it is not too noisy he may nap at her house, or walk the four blocks to his own house. Most of the men will follow the same pattern, and when they awake at four o'clock in the afternoon they will return to work, stroll downtown, or return to the *winkel*.

Many men drop in the *winkel* throughout the day. Most are marginal to the group[13] of about 15 men who frequent the *winkel* regularly and have good relations with one another. All the men are different, or at least they try to be. Each projects a certain image and supports a particular identity, perhaps as a man of streetcorner letters or through the tilt of a cap perched jauntily on the head or a clever way of turning a phrase or proverb. Their life styles are different too; but, similar enough to allow convergence and compatability in the *winkel* context.

Mr. Geld arrives most weekdays at 2:15 in the afternoon, just when *winkel* traffic is slowing down and most of the men are leaving. He is a soft spoken man of about 45 years who works as a repairman for the shipyards. His demeanor suggests a man of reason; a "gentleman," neither rude nor boisterous, disinterested in the gossip around him. He consciously comes to the *winkel* after lunch to avoid the crowds. In this atmosphere he can relax, unbothered by the prying eyes that search for a bit of useful gossip. He feels the more people know about you, the more they can hurt you, and that black people are especially fond of manipulating one another through gossip and story-telling. He is given to philosophical musing and, pointing to his skin, often says "this color is not good" (*disi boeba no boen*), thereafter launching into the standard Caribbean metaphor of "crab antics" (see Wilson, 1973).

He claims that if one black man sees another getting ahead, he will do his best to drag him down through slander, or worse, through sorcery and curses. He avoids this by drinking his whiskey with a few acquaintances and avoiding the loose congeries of strangers that pass through the *winkel* and gather temporarily every morning and evening.

Mr. Geld makes about Sf 295 per month. He lives in the upstairs of a two-story house not far away and pays a monthly rent of forty-five guilders. This is very high for the area where cottages run on the average between eight and twenty-five guilders. He had been living with a woman until about three years ago, and now pays forty guilders a month in child support for his two offspring.

Asked if he has a woman now, he will say no, but go on to explain that he has a "servant" (*dienstmeisje*) who cooks for him, cleans house, and occasionally spends the night with him. He pays her a salary of Sf 50 per month and provides her with occasional cash prestations and goods. He does not choose to *waka-waka* (visit, usually a number of women) or become involved with other women for fear they would only get him in trouble with other men and women, place unreasonable demands on him, and siphon off his salary. Although he occasionally rides his motorcycle to the *winkel* in the evenings, he prefers to stay home with a drink while reading the paper and watching television.

On his days off as accountant Mr. Rijker may stop in for an hour or so before lunch. Usually he comes 3 or 4 nights a week. He makes a good salary, about Sf 350 per month. Something, however, about Mr. Rijker's interaction patterns and use of time distinguishes him from the other men. It has very little to do with how much money he makes but rather that Mr. Rijker is married and behaves as a married man.

Compared to the other men, Mr. Rijker devotes huge amounts of time to home and family. Not that he does that much when home; his wife and her frequently visiting sister, mother and aunt see to all the household chores while the six children run messages, do odd jobs and repairs. Yet, he is often home, and when he goes to the *winkel* he neither stays as long nor spends as much money as the other men.

Because he does not invest time and energy at the *winkel,* Mr. Rijker is considered by the men to be marginal to the group of regulars. They claim "he never comes here," when actually he spends a good deal of time there. By a sort of self-serving mythology he is subtly excluded from full participation and membership in the gathering. He is not "one of the boys" in a very obvious sense and challenges group concepts of masculinity by his behavior. He cannot freely buy drinks and symbolically reaffirm his friendship, nor can he take off on a moment's notice for action miles away, nor can he engage in the sexual foreplay and dalliance that spices *winkel* life. If the men in the *winkel* have "manly flaws" (Liebow, 1967), Mr. Rijker points out that not all men have them.

Mr. Rijker's woman — his wife — also has a license to admonish him when he goes astray. She can legally demand more money for upkeep of herself, children and household affairs. Her female blood relatives — mother, aunt and two sisters, always in close contact — regularly, and playfully, if the indescretion is not serious, censure Mr. Rijker for imprudent behavior. One afternoon when he did imbile too much, and in the bedlam of *winkel* entertainment got captivated by the buxom charms and repartee of a young lady flirting about the *winkel,* word got back home carried by one of the neighborhood women who stopped in to make a purchase. He received a tongue lashing from the assembled women — mostly ridicule — emphasizing that he was a gullible male whose pockets would be emptied by a conniving (and competitive) young thing. In Suriname this is known as *"fom-fom nanga mofo,"* literally a "beating with the mouth." The men who gather at the *winkel* regularly warn one another of this danger.

About 10 o'clock every morning a group of young men in their late teens gathers on the corner outside the *winkel.* The older men (24 and older) never stay outside, but remain inside; the teenagers, however, move freely between the public world and the *winkel* arena. This movement in space is quite reflective of their *winkel* status and will be pursued in the section dealing with *winkel* recruitment.

There are six older teenagers, all from the neighborhood, and every midmorning, through the day, and into the evening they can be found here on the corner or in one of the adjacent back yards. They are all unemployed, and claim that the low salaries being paid do not make it worth their while to work. They all have high inspirations. Not one has more than an elementary school education. They claim that even if they went to school suitable jobs would not be available for them. Often they speak of going to Holland, both for the opportunities and the excitement. An East Indian controlled government was in power then, and many Creoles felt the pinch, especially when a favor needed to be done.[14]

The boys supplement their meager incomes by doing temporary odd jobs, soliciting food and money from their maternal relatives in the area, getting a guilder or two from a working sister, occasionally engaging in petty theft, and being present at auspicious moments when the men in the *winkel*, either on payday or when in a jolly mood, buy them a beer.

Given their ages it is not surprising that all the young men live in roughly the same arrangement; all with kin, either mother or mother's sister. All their siblings are present. One fellow has brought in his lover as well. However, this is not an ideal situation and as soon as he gets a job he will search for a small house and move out. The other fellows all mate extra-residentially with female age-mates in the neighborhood and as yet have no children.

The young men are all dressed in clean shirts and pressed slacks. All are considered well mannered and pleasant, although one of them has a reputation of being a thief. He does not steal in the neighborhood and so is not strongly censured or condemned, although watched suspiciously.

When it is available, and they have the money, they occasionally smoke marijuana in the back yards under the trees. More frequently they drink beer. The adult men in the *winkel* do not really know what marijuana is, other than that the media tell them it is bad. They are not interested and do not criticise the youths on this count. The marijuana itself, sold usually in the quantity of two joints for Sf 5, is of poor quality and is usually cut with vegetable greens. The boys buy only from trusted pushers who get their goods from Holland or Brazil and make the rounds from neighborhood to neighborhood. Marijuana is illegal in Suriname.

Gambling is a major youthful preoccupation and takes up a considerable portion of the time spent on the street. At innumerable corners in the area games of cards and dice are continually in progress, with players joining and leaving them in a steady stream. Others stand up behind the players, sometimes merely to spectate or else to bet among themselves on the outcome of the game. In the *winkels* the boys occasionally play dominoes, almost always with an audience, many of whose members are themselves committed financially to the game.

The boys infrequently go downtown to patronize the cafes, retaurant-beer joints, record shops, and other places of congregation. Better off and better educated youths (middle school or high school) usually spend their time in the city. Clerks, salesgirls, students, and the leisured can be seen hob-nobbing with the returnees from Holland, easily identified by their gaudy European trappings. The fellows who stand outside the *winkel* are much more comfortable in the neighborhood environment with its known safe places, faces and expectations than in hectic downtown Paramaribo (Brana-Shute, G., 1978).

These are some of the men who congregate at the *winkel*; Russel the custodian, unemployed teenagers, Schill the journalist, Marcell the lumberman, Geld the repairman, and Rijker the clerk. Of course there are other regulars. The closest knit group within the winkel consists of Elder, the 66 year old retired government functionary and now a part time clerk; van Kanten, an educated but alcoholic accountant; Charlie the auto mechanic; Frankie the unemployed cook; Toriman, the unemployed writer; Willem the cab driver; Chris the tour guide; Tony, a sometime employee at an orange crating factory; Jules the welder, and Mr. Bunker a lower-range civil servant. One, or some, or all of these men are sometimes or always at the *winkel*.

B) *Friendship and Mutual Aid*

Apart from the relaxation and drinking to be had the men provide positive services for one another. The favors proffered are for sustaining and maintaining *winkel* participation by those men who choose to partake.

The men ask few favors of one another and expect little help outside the *winkel*. Only rarely, and only between the best of friends (*mati*), does aid and assistance extend beyond the *winkel* to cover personal debts and material needs. If one is a member of the group that gathers here it is because he has established a good reputation. He does not mooch drinks, try to over-exploit the social, economic or political contacts of others, or gossip or pry into the affairs of the fellows. Should he be without means, others with money will see him through the rough days. However, this support is only to maintain the man's in-*winkel* behavior; that is, to allow him to buy drinks and tobacco so that he may participate in the group's interaction in a place that requires capital. This flow of aid is not without end; it is expected that the dependent party will reestablish himself and become self-sufficient soon.

Two examples follow. One shows how Frankie, a regular participant of good repute, activated a temporary *winkel* support fund to get him through troubled economic times. The second deals with Marcus, a non-member, who tried the same thing.

Frankie was employed as a cook at a lumber camp upriver from Albina on the border with French Guiana. He came to the *winkel* every weekend and frequently on weekdays during the rainy season when the jungle was difficult to work. One day he was told by his boss that part of the lumber camp would be sent up river to cut new grounds and that he was to go as their cook.

Frankie refused for, as he put it, he did not want to live in the jungle like a Bush Negro. Except for monthly furloughs, the new camp would deny him access to Paramaribo. Indignant, he quit, and for four weeks, before he found work as a part-time carpenter, his *winkel* needs were cared for by the *winkel* regulars. Everybody thought his behavior was justified; nobody wanted to work in the jungle or, perhaps more accurately, nobody wanted to be away from the city. His mother fed and clothed him, and there was always someone present at the *winkel* to provide conversation and something to drink. There were no grumblings as he did not over-indulge himself on the free liquor nor in any way flaunt his access to friendly aid. Frankie was expected to behave moderately, find work and reinstate himself.

Frankie had provided for others also when they were down and out. There were no tabs kept on Frankie's account and, unless he specifically asked for Sf 10 or Sf 15, he paid nothing back. His closer friends supported him more than the others, and those of them with more money supported him more than those with minimal funds.

Marcus, on the other hand, tried the same thing. His reputation was not nearly as good as Frankie's; he was considered unreliable and a gossip to boot. Scarcely a penny did he ever give his old mother, but squandered it on his pleasures. Marcus never bought for others but was ready and quick to accept a gift. He was not considered one of the boys, because of his abrasive demeanor and because he spent his time in many other *winkels,* potentially gossiping.

When he was laid off his low-paying job as a road worker for the Public Works Department he tried to activate an intra-*winkel* support network. At first help came in fits and starts with much grumbling, until one Saturday Marcus arrived at the *winkel* slightly drunk. He began pestering Charlie and Marcell to buy him a *djogo* (liter bottle of beer). Irritated with his lack of manners and past record, both refused. Marcus was aware of Marcell's quick temper and concentrated on the milder and less formidable 130 pound Charlie. Unable to stand the badgering, but getting no help from the other men, Charlie departed for home a few short paces down the street. Undaunted, Marcus entered Charlie's house without his knowing and continued pleading for beer. Charlie said nothing as Marcus helped himself to an open beer and proceeded to finish it all. Discomforted by the icy silence and lack of beer, Marcus left.

Charlie told this story at the *winkel* the next week, and everyone agreed that indeed Marcus was a *saka-saka* (low life). Word spread quickly that Marcus was no good (*takroe*) and by no means should anyone buy him anything. Marcus' participation tapered off during the next three weeks until now he drops by only occasionally on Saturday afternoons — and buys his own beer. He is greeted in a guarded manner by the men and his presence triggers cautious behavior on the part of the men present. The men have learned to laugh at the insincerity of quasi-intimate relationships, to admire performances of strength and to mock the inauthenticity of fools.

Friendship is not everything it is said to be. There is a proverb in Suriname — one of many — that penetrates the realities of male friendship deeper than the men's romantic accounts of brotherhood through thick and thin. Sometimes friendship does not and cannot stand up. The men know it, and in defense there is an unspoken rule to guide intra-*winkel* behavior: *Joe moesoe de boen nanga soema ma' joe no moesoe foe poeroe joe bere gi den* (You must get along with people but not tear out your insides for them).

Winkel regulars will admit that this proverb guides their relationships and even sets the shape and quality of friendships. People must always keep something secret and apart for themselves. No one is to be told or given everything. Someday the relationship, under strain neither man could foresee nor cope with, will break apart, as all do, and the information once given in good faith, the sentiment invested in a warm relationship, will be used against you. There are good friends who hang out together in the *winkel* and elsewhere, and who genuinely help each other and get along well, but they have not made a commitment to each other that they may someday be unable to meet.

A request for extra-*winkel* aid between two of the *winkel* regulars almost upset a good friendship. Schill was evicted from his house for nonpayment of rent during his hard times. He could not stay at his ex-woman's because she was seeing another man. His girl friend was living in a small house with her blood kin. Schill's sister was married to a respectable businessman and Schill could not expect her to take him in.

Schill asked Marcell if he could stay at his house and after some hesitation Marcell agreed. At this particular point Marcell had just moved out of his aunt's house and set up residence with his favorite current woman. Schill slept on the couch in the sitting room while Marcell and the women slept in the bedroom attic. Morning, Marcell went early to work while the woman stayed home. Schill slept late before going out. It was, by local standards, a most suspicious relationship.

Soon accusations began to fly as Marcell accused Schill of trying to seduce his woman. The neighbors assumed the worst and were spreading stories. Topics once enjoyed in the context of banter and joviality became sharp indictments. Behind Schill's back, Marcell ridiculed Schill's high manners (*he maniri*) and occasional pretentious demeanor.

Fearing ever worse trouble with Marcell and shame at the *winkel* as the charges began to spread, Schill reluctantly borrowed Sf 400 and moved into an inexpensive pension. The temporary breakdown of the dyad was re-established when they reverted to their previous *winkel* relationship.

In all, interaction among regulars is easy going. A fellow drops by and strolls to the table or counter where his buddies are congregated. Drinks — bottles of beer, rum and whiskey — lie about and the new arrival must merely yell to the barkeep for a glass. The men never share a glass or drink directly from the bottle. He then can sit down, pour a drink and enter into a conversation — or change it — at any point. When the bottle is dispatched he may or may not buy a refill, but has the privilege to take another drink. The exchange of cigarettes and snacks assumes the same arrangement.

When on the corner, the relationships a man has with all the other men present are not of the same intensity. In a sense, within the *winkel* group each man has his own personal network determined by degree of closeness and compatability. In the center are those people, one or two, that he considers his good friends — *mati* — and calls them by that title. These men are usually the same age, economic status and have roughly the same domestic arrangements. They are in daily face to face contact if the situation permits and they alone, of all the men at the *winkel*, "travel" together. Goods and services are regularly exchanged between them and no tally is kept — assuming of course that a somewhat general balance is maintained in the long run. With good friends one can discuss some more delicate problems without fear of him leaking information to damaging sources, turn to him for aid in a crisis, rely on for a favor and impose upon anytime, day or night, at work or off, when he is with a woman or not.

Towards the fringes of a man's *winkel* network are his acquaintances, persons with whom he is on good terms, drinks and debates with and can expect no attack — verbal or otherwise — no unanticipated blow to his reputation or pocketbook. The relationships are not in-depth but they are genuine, safe and pleasant.

Collectively, all of these personal networks within the *winkel*, juxtaposing friends and acquaintances, mesh to give temporary form and spirit to the *winkel* group. In the *winkel* context, it is difficult to distinguish friend from acquaintance for any one person since the men try hard not to single out one from their midst as someone special and apart. In the irregular tempo of *winkel* gatherings the group-networks of all the men occillate about the corner.[15]

Of course their total personal networks are not bounded by *winkel* walls but extend into the neighborhood and beyond. This outer fringe, ever changing in composition, is the realm of the person who deserves only simple recognition — a nod of the head, a hello — or worse, the enemy, those who seek to aggressively exploit or hurt you and yours.

The general impression here is one of a broad matrix of over-lapping networks in which the *winkel* group are constantly, though irregularly, meeting with one another on the corner. Within this circumscribed area one knows his friends and the degree of commitment he can expect from his acquaintances. It is remarkable that given the tempo and rhythm these men live by and the sentiments they share, the *winkel* group is so highly integrated with each man in every other man's network, though the degree of involvement varies. Outside of the *winkel* the overlap is considerably less, even non-existent. To be a recognized member of the *winkel* regulars means to expect some support when times are depressed. To be an outsider, even if the group outsider should live right next door to the *winkel*, does not qualify one for support, except perhaps one beer bought grudgingly by the weakest willed of those present.

C)   *Strangers, Gossip, and Reputation*

The *winkel* is home base for these men; rarely do they leave it to explore possibilities elsewhere.

Strangers entering the *winkel* are regarded with caution and suspicion. The alien is watched closely and, after his departure, is discussed at length until his identity is established in either fact or theory.

Men are paid fortnightly or monthly. During these times they congregate at the *winkel* with greater frequency and for a longer duration, many times spending a good deal of their wages within a week. Waiting for the next paycheck, a man tapers off his drinking, buys the less expensive beer, and tries to borrow money from one of his women. He also attempts to activate his *winkel* support networks.

Payday is also the time that young women without men, ex-concubines and lovers flit in and out of the *winkel* to locate ex- and future lovers. Men who are without money also engage in a similar tactic around payday. The following story, about a man without funds who is seeking money, is often told about "strangers" who enter a *winkel*.

A person enters a *winkel* and notices another man or men drinking and spending money. He watches for a few moments and sizes up the situation; how much money the man has, with who he is drinking, and, among other things, his general deportment. The seeker then approaches the man and engages him in a rapid and intense conversation on a topic of common interest (developments in

Holland, political news, ethnic problems) upon which the two men will probably be in agreement. If the conversation is agreeable, the seeker may ask to have a drink. The *winkel* men are especially leary of this play and only infrequently engage strangers in conversations. After the encounter the seeker asks the proprietor or someone else if the man lives in the area, has a job and comes to the *winkel* often. If the answers are satisfactory the seeker often returns. Some people, it is claimed, spend no money but have a set routine of *winkels* they visit.

These "strangers" often try to mount a "hustle" and, depending on their virtuosity in manipulating imagery and relationships, may or may not succeed. His rewards can be various; he can provide entertainment for himself and others, acquire a drink, or, perhaps existentially, reinforce an identity in a drama of his own making. Failing, he may do nothing more than "hustle" himself.

These daily routines of ambiguous sociability require a steady feedback of sounds (usually grunts indicating yes or no) and gestures (nods, eye and hand movements, explosive laughter or earsplitting "jupes") all of which are responsible for determining the nature of the continuing drama. The presentation is received by the audience and if they respond positively they bestow the gift of reality; to do otherwise is to negate the stranger's scenario, deny his identity and certainly cause him to leave indignant and insulted, commenting derisively on the nature of mankind.

Either result of the encounter is supportive of the men. The play has allowed them to determine who was "for real" and authentic. If the hustle failed at least the group regulars were enriched by the insight into another personality, were entertained and had its own unity and cohesion symbolically reinforced by the unsuccessful performer. Normally porous group boundaries seemed, at the moment of denying admittance to the stranger, very solid and exclusive indeed.

New and unexplored places are avoided as well. One can always be approached in an alien *winkel* or drinking bar and, without the comfort and security of friendly faces, be easily manipulated or victimized. Even in the safety of the *winkel* the men will cover their glass with a coaster and ask a crew member to keep an eye on it while they temporarily depart. This precaution prevents a stranger from placing a poison or charm in the drink.

By the standards of the *winkel* men, Jules has spead his inter-personal contacts far and wide and this can only lead to trouble, for his all too frequent contact with strangers. This opinion was confirmed when a near-disaster befell Jules. One of the frequent and wide spread means of destroying or gaining control of someone is through poison, usually surreptitiously slipped into a drink while in a public place. As a safeguard against this, Jules visited a magician (*bonoeman*) and secured a protective charm (*tapoe*) which would inform him of the imminent danger of poison.

Jules enjoys a special reputation as a singer (*singiman*). He attends all night wakes (*dede oso*) held by Creoles for their deceased and, drawing on his extensive repertoire of hymns, leads the mourners in song. He also holds down a job, and it is not an unusual week when he spends 4 or 5 nights singing from 10 p.m. until sunrise followed by a day of work.

One day after a particularily busy week of singing *dede oso* Jules was walking from work and was hailed from a nearby *winkel* by someone he didn't recognize. He entered and was offered a glass of rum by men who explained that they had witnessed his singing that week and now wished to praise him with a toast. Jules was suspicious and, although cordial, hesitated to drink. He surveyed the room trying to place everyone. With prompting he lifted the glass to drink. Suddenly his hand began to quiver and the bottom of the glass shattered, spilling the poisoned rum on the table. Without a word Jules arose and left. The *tapoe* had saved him.

When Jules later told us the story in the *winkel* he noted that he had been getting careless, entering places filled with strangers without thinking. For his own health he decided to limit his drinking only to a circle of close friends and to sing *dede oso* only for people he knew very well. The men all nodded their heads in silent approval. A few gave reinforcing stories of similar plights. Jules closed the conversation by pointing out that the Creoles engage too much in "crab antics" (*kraboe politiek*); when one Creole sees another getting ahead, enjoying a special reputation, or possessing something he himself does not have, he will try and "pull him down."

Normally when a person with whom one is not well acquainted enters the *winkel*, the men alter their conversation momentarily to avoid reference to gossip or stories about people outside their immediate group. Gossip is not for all ears, and women are especially suspected of maliciously using any bit of information they hear or, at the least, ridiculing men whom they think have nothing better to do than sit around and gossip.

One weekday evening Marcell was involved in a deep discussion with a gardener from the neighborhood. Both men are dark skinned *nengre* and by all outward manifestations are lower-class. With people of these social characteristics, especially in a *winkel* atmosphere, *Sranan Tongo* is the expected language; Dutch would be "putting it on" (*bigi fasi*). However, the discussion dealt with the pro's and con's of independence for Suriname and both men lapsed into Dutch to lend the air of formality to the debate (not, as some think, because *Sranan Tongo* is incapable of expressing such complicated thoughts). The gardener's Dutch was halting and riddled with mistakes while Marcell was speaking fluently.

At this point a woman from the neighborhood and her two teenage daughters entered the *winkel*. In mock surprise the two girls turned and stared wide-eyed at Marcell. They laughed. Snickering, they remarked to each other that two black men were conversing in Dutch. The woman kept her back turned. Marcell stopped mid-sentence and stalked furiously over to the two girls. He admonished them, reminding them that they were as black as he, no better than he, and that, if he wanted to, he could speak Dutch. One of the girls casually dipped her head and remarked that she was brown, while the other accused Marcell of being a Bush Negro (Marcell *na wan Djuka, jere*) because Bush Negroes are uniformly darker skinned than the mixed-blood Creoles. Also, city Creoles (*foto soema*) by and large consider themselves more sophisticated and worldy than the deprecating stereotype of the unlettered, primitive Bush Negroes. Marcell exploded in rage and, turning to the mother who was nervously ignoring the scenario, asked how her daughter's "marijuana baby" was. The woman grabbed her bundle and bodily ushered the two girls out the door. Marcell had countered victoriously with a piece of gossip, alluding to a "shame story" (*sjen tori*) that brought more loss of respect to them than their remarks had brought to him. The "shame story" referred to one of the teenage girls who had smoked marijuana with a group of friends one evening and had had intercourse with one of them when "high." Finding herself pregnant she claimed she could not remember with whom she had slept that night. The child is now unsupported and unrecognized by its father.

One should be wary of excessive bravado. A member of the group will quickly be cut down to size and belittled if he operates outside or above the boundaries of the status the group has defined as appropriate. This is another aspect of "crab antics."

Schill, for instance, is allowed great latitude. He may give forth in Dutch on the most complicated of issues ranging from the revision of the tax structure to knowledgeable insights into various neighborhood personalities. He is allowed the privilege of unsolicited advice and negative criticism. Although one of the group, Schill is its high status member. A combination of education, contacts, and wealth, when he has it, sees to this. There is also the element of charisma — Schill has many of or plays upon the attributes of a " good man," as the men at the *winkel* define it.

Others, however, should mind their status and adjust their behavior accordingly. One day hapless, unlettered Russel did not. Russel had just received his monthly paycheck, plus a bonus that was promised all government workers during the labor strikes of the preceding months. Going straight to the largest department store in the city, Russel squandered every penny on an expensive radio-cassette tape player. Not one guilder was left over for his woman Betty or to buy alcohol for himself and his companions during the coming days.

Russel marched proudly into the *winkel* with his new possession and, holding it fondly, placed it on the glass case. Not a sound was made by the men; they were all eyes. Ordering a beer, he began busily pressing buttons and twirling knobs. He obviously had no idea of what he was doing.

After a few more moments of fumbling, Pinas, a crew member, who had held a long term grudge against Russel, in proper *winkel* abeyance, arose and walked to Russel. In a remark absolutely unrelated to anything said during the entire morning, Pinas insinuated that Russel was a big-bellied weakling, knew nothing of the art of fisticuffs, and could never defend himself or his close ones if he needed. Russel bowed his head and said nothing. The other men, Marcell, Schill, Frankie and van Kanten, all regulars in good standing, quietly looked on. Further references were made to Russel's slovenly appearance and lack of manners. Not a mention was made of the new radio. Russel was insulted mightily. Finally, in a last outburst, Pinas said that Russel did not know how to operate the piece and, furthermore, was too dumb to learn. Pinas stalked away and contentedly seated himself in the corner on the periphery of the gathered men. Russel walked out of the *winkel,* humiliated.

It is not that one cannot bring "status elevating" possessions to the *winkel.* Elder, the old clerk, clever storyteller and crew member in good standing, once brought in an outrageous shocking pink portable record player, and with great pomp and showmanship played three old and bruised records at ear-splitting pitch all evening. No challenge was made.

Russel has a reputation in the neighborhood as everyone does. He is considered to be an unlettered and unskilled simpleton. He is fat, sloppy and only occasionally washed. He has little money and his experiences with women demonstrate neither quantity, quality nor an abundance of offspring. He is the brunt of jokes and literally salivates when he spies an available bottle of alcohol, in which he regularly overindulges and makes a worse fool of himself. He gossips about his woman and even describes the failures and ecstasies of his latest sexual experience with her. This is not a good reputation. Yet, Russel is harmless and the men enjoy the buffoonery. But, beware Russel the court-jester, the simpleton who seems to do the reverse or opposite of everyone else. There are dangers here, for the weak possess certain powers, the principal one being the ability to strip off the pretensions of those possessed of higher reputation or status.

Russel challenges, daily, everything the men say they are or should be. In some respects this behavior in the *communitas* of the *winkel* atmosphere is refreshing and tolerated, for certainly the collective presence and behavior of the other men present vindicates their belief in themselves and in the others as "good men." Temporary and not terribly threatening status reversals are tolerated everywhere. But the radio — this fine material piece with buttons, lights, switches and the power to pull in words and stories from near and far, to garner experiences, as well as impress certain women — was the red line. *Winkel* equilibrium had to be reestablished, and it was.

These contests are an everyday occurance in the area and usually obtain an audience. Indeed, the audience present often determines the style and content of the verbal exchange. The ability to "talk" therefore — including story telling, arguing, trading insults and conning or making a fool of the opponent — is a highly cultivated art. Talking also permits the men to express their feelings and ideas through a language and street argot rich in imagery and metaphor in a manner which rationalizes and explains their actions.[16] One major function of the "story" — which can deal with absolutely anything — is that it makes both participants and audience "feel good." Quite regularly a highly personalized tale will be delivered for exactly that reason.

D) *Interaction: Recruitment and Expulsion*

The ad hoc gathering of *winkel* regulars is not a corporate unit nor do the men recognize it as such. Fluidity and change characterize these personal relationships as they do with family, household and occupational relationships. By dint of desire, duress or whimsy a man can alter the composition of his network and completely drop out of the *winkel* crew. There is no fanfare or ritual to mark his departure. He may still have contact with the regulars on a one to one basis, but his interactions — the intensity and sentiment of these relations — would not take place within *winkel* walls.

Entry into a *winkel* group is fluid as well — once the interested party overcomes the onus of stranger. Providing one has an acceptable reputation and in his *winkel* participation demonstrates good intentions, he is welcomed. A "manly" stature is a prerequisite, though the enumeration of such qualities often varies from individual to individual. In effect, one is already in possession of his "reputation" before gaining regular entry. The newcomer transacts his image with the regulars and sets forth his "style" for group consumption. His position in the occupational hierarchy and official skills at the workplace will go unnoticed, perhaps indefinitely, until he has made himself known.[17] Style and presentation of self in the *winkel* setting is enormously important and one performs in the way he stands, walks, talks, dresses and otherwise self-consciously conducts himself. At once, a "player" creates a role for self and others, develops a situation in which he chooses to exist and provides entertainment.

To trait list a profile would be an impossible chore; indeed, despicable qualities for one might be applauded in another. Unless a man is an obvious and recognized threat to *winkel* unity — picking fights, shirking drink buying responsibilities or interfering with another's private life — a sort of "provincial morality" (Gans, 1962) is at work that allows each man's characteristics to be woven into his own constellation of appreciated attributes. The streetcorner self, whether the definition is supported by a huge capacity to hold drink, spin yarns and tell tales, comment on local and national events with insight born of experience (*ondrofeni*) or sit quietly and appreciate the antics of others are all incorporated into the on-going activities and sentiments of group life.[18]

The *winkel* gathering provides no explicit rite of passage, no badge of identity to the initiate. After close scrutiny and subtle discussion of this qualities, the outsider, be he 25 or 55, finds himself absorbed into conversations and the ritual of drinking and story telling. First, however, he must learn the lore of the neighborhood and familiarize himself with identities that each man manages and maintains. This all comes in time, as he associates stories with faces and identifies the important or unique personages of the neighborhood. (This assumes that he already knows the national lore, politics, ethnic groups, etc. — and feels the same way about these topics as the rest of the men in the *winkel* do.) Neither his interaction patterns nor sentiments should be in conflict with or contradictory to the internal organization of the group. Three examples follow. The first deals with recruitment into the *winkel*; the second with an individual's departure, and the third with how one re-establishes contact with the *winkel* after a temporary absence. The third example is interesting as it demonstrates the "shock-absorber" function of the *winkel* as sanctuary.

Toriman was employed as a free lance writer until his main buyer folded. Until this time he had only occasionally been to the *winkel*, and then only for a beer or two. His only contact with the crew was a tenuous acquaintanceship with Schill. Though unemployed, he continued to stay on at his woman's house and took his meals with her. They were very fond of one another. Mornings he took the bus into town to his political party headquarters to spend his time reading the newspapers and listening to the radio. He belonged to a different Creole political party than most of the Creoles at the *winkel*, but there was talk of them working in coalition in the forthcoming election.

On his way home, Toriman would walk through the city to meet people and chat, pick up bits of information and simply engage in the most popular of Surinamese pastimes, walking and talking (*koirie*). He had to pass the *winkel* and often stopped in until finally he began showing up daily. Toriman was recognized as being a raconteur, the equal, if not the superior of Schill and from the beginning assumed a high status position in the group. He still had money to buy drinks, offered intelligent commentary, told a good story, was pleasant and polite, minded his own business and, in short, fit the definition of an acceptable man. Toriman engaged all the crew in banter, salutation and drinking. When his funds finally gave out he was kept in drinks by his new found fellows. The whole process took no more than four weeks.

It is as easy to depart from the group as it is to enter it. Group organization allows for periodic recurrent or non-recurrent absence as well as final departure.

Although a crew member, Mr. Rijker was marginal to all the men. Domestic demands forced him to devote considerable time and money to his family of legal wife and children. Stories about the academic success of his children, of whom he is very proud, triggered no response from the assembled men. Their only contact with many of their own children was through the money they funnel to their mothers. An occasional Sunday morning stroll with one of their children was often the totality of contact these men had with the children they had produced through visiting relationships.

Without his wife's knowledge, Mr. Rijker had established credit at the *winkel* for his drinking. After turning over his paycheck to his wife (something that the men living in concubinage or engaged in visiting relationships do not do) he would use his surreptitiously gained overtime pay to slowly whittle away at the charges which usually increased faster than he could pay them. This was fine with Chung, providing regular remittances were made.

For some time Mr. Rijker had been behaving strangely. He was more taciturn than usual and stories about his children were no longer heard. It was an old woman who lived next door to the Rijkers who first cast light on the subject. She had noticed over the past three months that Rijker's daughter had not been undertaking her monthly washing of blood-stained menstrual underwear and hanging them on a separate clothes line to dry (such garments are treated with special care and are tended to only by the wearer). She investigated and discovered that the daughter was pregnant by a fellow up the street.

Rijker had always wanted his daughter married before conceiving but she followed the conventional ways of the neighborhood. To make matters worse she mated with a fellow whose family had no respect and who could only bring shame to her family. Under no circumstances would they allow her to live with the fellow and were even considering not suing for child support. During this same period, Mr. Rijker's father was going blind and would need expensive medical treatment. Mr. Rijker would soon face a mountain of bills.

At the end of the month Chung began asking everyone for money. Normally he would have let it go longer, but Chung pressured Mr. Rijker realizing he was now a bad credit risk. With family debts increasing, Mr. Rijker could not easily continue his drinking. Chung thought it pointless to extend more credit. Pestering Rijker unmercifully and demeaning him in front of the group, Chung made Rijker uneasy. The men did not like what was happening either; Rijker was a backslider, and suddenly all the things that distinguished him from them were brought sharply into focus. He was shamed both on account of his pregnant daughter (whom he had touted so highly — although the others knew better since one of the crew occasionally had intercourse with her) and his inability to pay his bills. He departed and did not show up again. Daily he could be seen entering and leaving his house; often he went to another *winkel* two blocks down the street to do his now occasional drinking. Mr. Rijker lives within sight of the *winkel*, but as custom would dictate, he was never visited at home. The group carried on affairs as usual, an occasional comment would be made about his family, his whereabouts or his daughter's behavior, but no one ventured over to his house to re-establish contact. Neither Rijker's presence nor, for that matter, anyone else's is instrumental to the survival of the group.

Another case is also instructive. A young man of 24, Richard lived with his mother's sister until he met Eleanor. They were immediately fond of one another and all parties concerned realized that their visiting relationship would develop into something more permanent.

Prior to his relationship with Eleanor, Richard spent a good deal of time in the *winkel* and, although interacting mostly with the older pre-*winkel* teenagers and the younger members of the *winkel* group (his age and slightly older), he was fast being absorbed into the full round *winkel* life. He was eminently eligible, always with some money in his pocket, being the proper age and possessing a friendly personality.

One thing, however, distinguished Richard from the other men. Although spending substantial sums at the *winkel*, he always set aside a bit for future acquisitions. Recently he bought an old used car for Sf 900. He was financially more imaginative and aggressive than most of the men his age and had designs on operating a private taxi service.

Eleanor's mother was in the districts and Eleanor, to pursue her career as nurse's aid and continue her education at night school, lived in Paramaribo with one of her mother's sisters. As a truck driver and part-time taxi driver, Richard's income was adequate to plan a future. Everyone was satisfied with his diligence and pleasant demeanor.

In proper form, Richard approached Josha, Eleanor's aunt, and asked to take Eleanor to live in concubinage (*libi makandra*). Josha sought the advice of her mother and everyone agreed that Eleanor's mother would sanction the union. Richard promised to marry Eleanor after he saved enough money to build and furnish a proper house. For the time being they would live in a small house loaned to Richard by his sister.

For seven months they lived together, both working and saving. Eleanor became pregnant, and plans were made for a wedding after she recovered from childbirth. The house was near completion and relatives would loan furnishings.

Richard spent less and less time at the *winkel*. One or two days a week after work he would stop by for conversation and a drink. His participation in group affairs, however, was flagging measurably. He rarely engaged in the reciprocal drinking. Saturdays found him hard at work on his new house.

Tragedy struck when Eleanor was killed in a traffic accident. The two families gathered and performed the rituals to usher her safely to the spirit world. Richard, distraught and grieving, swore never to look at another woman. He disposed of the nearly completed house.

During the second major period of mourning (the first 6 months after the funeral) Richard continued working. He took his meals and had other services performed at his sister's. He had always been on good terms with Eleanor's family and stopped by frequently to visit them. They helped him immensely in the trying days of the wake by rotating (older women) to stay the night with him. (During the eight day period after death the house is to be kept open and the principal mourners are not to be left alone.) During this period Eleanor's family acted beyond normal protocol (in fact, they acted like consanguines) and cared for Richard who was alone in Suriname except for one sister.

The older women in Eleanor's family discounted Richard's pledges never to look at another woman. They all knew better, both about men and the human condition. Slowly, Richard's visits dwindled off to occasional greetings and accidental meetings (Brana-Shute, R. and G. Brana-Shute, 1977).

He returned ever more frequently to the *winkel,* and in the absence of interaction with his lover participated more intensely with the men. At the same time he reestablished residence with his maternal aunt. His domestic responsibilities only involved sleeping there more often than not, eating the afternoon meal and remitting rent every two weeks.

Wilson (1974), although he did not describe the process in detail, found this same sort of "household-*winkel* oscillation" and alternating intensification and de-intensification of peer group contacts. He states (1974: 183): "The actions and settings of the crew are independent of the household, but as a man comes closer to forming his own household, he becomes much less dependent on his crew. Relations become less intense . . . " For Richard, his departure from the *winkel* was short-circuited. The *winkel* absorbed the shock of Richard's abruptly disturbed interaction. From his new *winkel* base, Richard began visiting young ladies and returned to a not uncommon lifestyle.

Men cycle into and out of the *winkel* for a variety of reasons; financial, domestic, situational, location in space etc. One of the determinants guiding recruitment, loss, and replenishment of personnel is age. The men who gather here regularly and share a common pool of temporary resources range in age from 24 to 62. Other *winkels* in Paramaribo are constituted similarly. Regulars are rarely younger than their early twenties or beyond their late sixties.

There are many teenage males in the neighborhood; fully 49 per cent of the total population of Suriname is below the age of 16. Groups of males between 16 and 20 stand on streetcorners, sit in back yards, go for walks, attend movies and dances, and engage in banter with young women in their spare time. The teenagers in this neighborhood have more spare time than other young people from better off neighborhoods who go to school.

The young men of lower-class background in *Frimangron* do not patronize the slick European oriented bars and cafes of downtown. They prefer the neighborhood. Besides the teenagers described above, there are five or six others in or around the *winkel* at least once a day. To a man they are unemployed, have no schooling past the elementary grades, know no trade, have little money and are supported by their consanguineal kin.

The boys have tastes apart from the older men's. They enjoy the outdoor sights and sounds of the neighborhood, and look to experience what the city has to offer. They attend dances held on weekends. At birthday parties held usually for older people they can be seen standing as a group. Movies and attendance at special events such as political rallies fill the bill. Teenagers from this neighborhood travel in all male groups.

Such young men are ineligible for *winkel* membership. Although young, their age alone would not bar them from membership. Age categories are flexible and, although there is the sanction of always showing respect to elders, the three generations are always in close and familiar contact. Age grade lines are not sharply defined. Money is a crucial entrance requirement for *winkel* pastimes.

Adam, 22 and part-time house painter, began to frequent the *winkel* prior to his decision to migrate to Holland. He engaged the men in debates on politics and admirably held his own. He discussed with maturity the topics of the day: ethnic competition, Holland, women and money. Although he moved with great ease between the teenagers and the men, he was slowly losing contact with his younger peers.

Other things were going on with Adam as well, all normal for a person at Adam's point in life. He was seeing a young woman on a visiting basis far more frequently than the casual liaisons established by his younger friends. He needed money to provide gifts and thus took on part-time jobs. He did not give any of his meager salary to his mother (in this case he was not expected to as adequate income came from other sources and she was an indulgent woman). Adam began spending his surplus at the *winkel*. Although he could not quite afford to bestow a pint of whiskey on the *winkel* men, he was able to provide for himself. The other teenagers had to wait until they collectively had enough money to buy a drink or else wait until someone offered.

In contrast, Adam was developing a pattern that would soon launch him into *winkel* life. He had established a good reputation there, had engaged a woman in a semi-permanent visiting relationship that would probably become concubinage and had gone to work. His salary, education and social background made him ineligible for higher circles but made him eminently suited for *winkel* membership.

For Adam, the *winkel* was the only place to regularly go and spend his leisure time. However, he was taken by the tales of bright lights and opportunities in Amsterdam and decided to migrate there and live with an aunt. Mother, girl friend and *winkel* pals remained behind. The other boys, who cannot or choose not to migrate, will eventually take their turn of *winkel* membership.

A *winkel* group is depleted as well as replenished, and one sees few men over 65 as regulars. This in part reflects the weakened physical constitution of old age. Heavy drinking takes it toll and many an old man has staggered home after being caught up in the joviality of a normal, sober afternoon at the *winkel*. The *winkel* men have an immense capacity for alcohol — truly astounding — but only occasionally are they bawdy or drunk. Moreover, older men do not have the financial resources of younger men. Only the Surinamese government and the larger businesses provide retirement pensions and these do not mount to much. There is also a government old age pension for all citizens over 70 that amounts to Sf 25 per month. Paramaribo is full of young competitive workers who decrease the older men's chances to supplement income with a part-time job.

As with the teenagers, old men can occasionally frequent the *winkel* and buy a bottle of beer or, just as likely, have a drink bought for them. However, they are unable to participate in the on-going exchange networks.

There are four broad categories of domestic relationships open for an elderly male that affect his participation in *winkel* life. He may be living in faithful concubinage or be married. Being older he will not have as many relationships with outside women and he thus contributes more time and money to this woman or wife. The children of previous unions are adult, thus freeing him from their support. Conjugal unions stabilize for older people, sometimes resulting in marriage in later years. Infrequently he may have dependent consanguines, usually sisters, of his age group that he must help support.

The older male may be living with consanguines, generally sisters, children, or collaterals further removed. In such cases he is expected to contribute either goods (money) or services (baby sitting, errands, etc.) to the household.

A man who lives with neither a woman nor relatives lives alone. However, he is still dependent on outsiders for services such as food, laundry and financial contributions. Although some men reside alone, it is misleading and inaccurate to consider their houses one-person households. Many are totally dependent on the services provided by non-residents who form a support network crucial to his survival.

If sick, destitute or without family the old man may be put away in an old folk's home as ward of the state. His needs are taken care of by an institution and his mobility is limited.

Many older men find their time and available resources commited to the maintenance of one household and its female head. Gone are the days when he could rely on the services of many women. An older man without a woman is a sorry and lonesome sight and an older man without money or contributions to make is not a welcome one. In his later years a man secures and consolidates his time and resources around one household and ventures very little into the young man's preserve of the *winkel*. In the absence of consanguines his age who might be dead or living elsewhere and with whom he has the closest geneological tie, the older man might choose to solidify his residential rights with a conjugal through marriage.

The men who gather in the *winkel* do not live in a state of poverty. They disburse their money in the *winkel*, with women (consanguines and affines) and on material goods that leave them little surplus. Their social relationships determine the distribution of the money they earn, no matter how much or how little. If the behavior of these men is to be somehow tied into a study of family structure and household composition it is far too simplistic to focus only on their position in the "occupational hierarchy." If the "family" is to be considered a "sub-system" in which the men as "breadwinners" link to the "larger system of on-going relationships" then the men here link together many such sub-systems and link each in a different manner to on-going society.

Many people in Paramaribo *are* poor. They have inadequate food, clothing and shelter. They do not enjoy nearly the degree of entertainment that the *winkel* men do. Poor people may be totally unemployed or perhaps run their lives and those dependent on them on less than Sf 50 or 60 a month; income from unreliable sources. In contrast, many of the men in the *winkel* spend Sf 100 a month on alcohol and tobacco.

Poor men cannot enjoy *winkel* pastimes. They drop in for drinks only when they have the money. If a man is not working for a salary it is usually the woman (either consanguineal or conjugal, although less often the latter if he makes no money) with whom he stays that sees to it that money enters the house by working part time, hawking fruits and vegetables, seeing other men, or waiting her turn in a rotating credit organization (*kas moni*). A man with no income is a liability quickly dispensed with.

These men are not eligible for *winkel* membership. Financially they are inadequate. Many times they are spotted by the *winkel* regulars as moochers who make the rounds of various *winkels* a few days after payday to absorb the overflow or on Saturdays when especially heavy drinking takes place.

The poorer men, when not at the *winkel*, drink in back yards or seek out birthday parties and wakes where food and alcohol are served. It is standard for Creoles to watch out for strangers who come to parties uninvited (*boroman*); they are only there to snoop, possibly steal and certainly to eat, drink, and leave (*njan, dringi, gowe*).

Males, principally middle class, by virtue of the type and variety of their social contacts and networks as well as their salaries, come only occasionally to the *winkel*. It should be recalled that, in terms of salaries, many of the "lower-class" *winkel* men make a good deal more money than their middle class counterparts. There is a good deal of salary overlap between the two groups. The *winkel* draws a heterogeneous Creole clientele and it comes as no surprise to see a poorer man in the same *winkel* with a successful blue collar worker or white collar clerk. Language and demeanor are polarized, yet the middle class man knows better than to act haughtily and arrogantly. Although there are obvious status distinctions between the clientele, the *winkel* is a place where the myth of social equality is fostered.

In contrast, the middle class male has liens on his resources that mitigate against a full blown *winkel* participation. Two crucial variables are time and money. The middle class male is more likely to be involved in a bureaucratic or assembly line job that requires strict adherence to a regimented time schedule. To avail himself of promotions, salary increases and fit into the general process of upward mobility he must comply with demands and use his time judiciously. *Winkel* men are not so concerned with this strategy; given their education and background many have progressed as far as they can go. (In the case of Schill who resorted to the *winkel* with his high education and so forth, his behavior could be considered a temporary strategy. He had temporarily — until there was a new opportunity — "sunk.")

It would also blemish the middle class man's propriety to hang out in a *winkel*. "Of course," people say, "he is a man and therefore destined to do this sort of thing occasionally," but a too frequent display of this sort of behavior could only bring shame and tarnish to a middle class reputation.

The middle class man is usually married, and aside from his work must devote time to wife and family. He is required to support his legal wife and children. Education must be paid for, clothes and books purchased, and a proper home environment created. He is involved in a long term, ongoing series of relationships that are sanctioned by law and custom. Regularly he is forced to consolidate his social and economic capital (See Whitten, 1965).

Most of the socializing middle class males do takes place in clubs, either those affiliated with his place of work or open through private membership. Parties with friends and relatives are important. Middle class men often take their wives along when going out. Their interaction patterns and the groups they form are on a scale far different from that of the *winkel* men.[19]

Although the *winkel* men prefer gathering at the *winkel*, there are other places where some of them occasionally go. They do not go as a group and only irregularly do they frequent other establishments. An enterprising person, usually a woman, can convert her back yard into a clandestine drinking "garden" (*sopi tenti*). Usually this results from capitalising on a building already there or from one especially built for a birthday celebration. Small places such as this abound, and some of the men have a favorite several blocks away.

One *sopi tenti* frequented by some of the men is a four-sided building with wood walls five feet high and a corrugated tin roof supported by ten foot poles. It measures about thirty feet with poured concrete floors and was built eight years ago to properly encase the dancing festivities for its owner's fiftieth birthday (a *bigi jari* or "big year").

Checkerboards, dominoes and playing cards are provided, as well as a record player which booms both Surinamese music and American "soul." All ages of men gather here to talk, drink and play games. The *tenti*, however, is more diversion than a common meeting ground for the men who regularly congregate at the *winkel*. Only a few from the *winkel* go there with any regularity and only when they are passing through that part of the neighborhood.

Charlie the auto mechanic lives next door to the *winkel* and owns a portable shuffle board game. Some of the men drop over nightly to pay a few turns, for Charlie is a friend and also sells beer from his refrigerator. However, there are usually too may teenagers about waiting their turn to play and the men drift back to the *winkel* where they find it more comfortable.

The men go to the movies, some two or three times a week. They usually go alone, neither with other *winkel* men nor women. (Teenagers go in groups while middle class men go with their wives.) The movies cost Sf .75 for the cheapest seats and are not prohibitively expensive. The preferred film genre is Hollywood "black gangster" or Kung Foo.

Professional prostitutes are rarely engaged by *winkel* men. There is really no need to seek out a street walker who nightly ply themselves in downtown Paramaribo. The *winkel* men have a number of women and spending Sf 7 tot Sf 15 for a visit with a prostitute is considered an injudicious use of money. When a man pays a prostitute for sexual services rendered, he then terminates the "single stranded" relationship. It is not long term or on-going and he very likely may never see her again. The relation is for one purpose only and then dissolved.

The men do divide up large amounts of money among the women with whom they have sexual relations (see Chapter 4). But these women are engaged in on-going, short or long term, multi-faceted and reciprocal relationships with the men. The men do not have sexual inercourse with these women every time they give them money nor do they give them money every time they have sexual intercourse. The relationship is a visiting relationship with rights and responsibilities recognized by both parties. The women provide services for the man; sex, food, laundry, a boost to his ego and male reputation, children, etc., while the male provides gifts, financial support and legitimacy for some of her children.

Couched in economic terms these male-female relatonships may lie dormant until one party or the other has need. The contact may be activated by either the male or the female, for females manipulate resource strategies as well as men. It is relatively easy to terminate the relationship if children have not resulted, otherwise, it endures in diminished form. The relationships have a time depth.

One thing emerges from looking at these men and others like them in

Paramaribo. They are lower-class in their orientation, pastimes, social relationships, life styles and use of time. They are not poor; being poor would deny them access to the *winkel* sub-culture. They have money but, for many of them, neither enough of it nor the appropriate skills to extricate themselves from a not totally unpleasant life. The children they father and the males who are now younger than they will be caught up in this life style that is based largely on subcultural traditions (the mating system), exclusion from macrostructural resources (education and prestigious jobs), and adaptation (reliance on a wide web of kin and friends for mutual support).

The relationships that each man forms with other men of the *winkel* group are loose, shifting, short term, and not totally committal. This same interaction pattern is replicated when men deal with women within the household group. There is no sharp bifurcation of interaction rate and style when men deal with men or women; both groupings replicate similar patterns and mutually reinforce one another.

E) *Men in Groups: Centrifugal and Centripetal Forces*

The 15 or so men who make up the *winkel* group of regulars are almost never all together at the same time. Far too many extra-*winkel* activities tying each male to his own time schedule and responsibilities mitigate against this.

Some men show up as regularly as clockwork, others erratically as schedules permit. In most cases, the men's presence or absence is dictated not by domestic commitments but by the spinning of their work cycles. After an absence, of hours or of weeks, one is never asked where he has been or what he was up to, even though this may have been a topic of discussion prior to his re-entry. The conversation goes on, concerning matters of the present and the Johnny-come-lately — about whom the men know all they have to know — is easily absorbed into matters of the moment.

Saturdays are busy (boisterous if Friday was payday) and the *winkel* is packed by 10 a.m. It is possible for the regulars present to assemble as a unit, for a long time, before they begin on their separate ways. This does not happen often and rarely are they seen sitting or standing in a discrete cluster. Two or three are seated at one table, another is standing at the counter and another talks outside with a passing woman. But the frequency, intensity and duration of their interaction, if viewed over a time span, distinguishes them from the passers-by.[20] The rules by which they play and the sentiment expressed in their conversation transforms them into a group apart from the others.

It might be that this has led some Caribbeanists to focus on the neatly clustered women and children who regularly congregate in their houses and yards. Men are not so neatly packaged. One must follow the movement of their relationships, sometimes a journey of fits and starts, of contacts hither and yon, dyads activated and deactivated, to grasp the nature of the groups they form. Time is an integral building block of social organization and should not be overlooked simply because it is more difficult to pin down than were it in the form of clubs, households, auxiliaries or other forms of recurrent congregations.

These drinking shops are important centers of the male world, and they provide a context in which males act out, socially and symbolically, matters which concern them most. The shops are forums where the men compete with each other in the proofs of their masculinity and where they seek to display and to acquire their reputations. The *winkel* is also the center of an established network of male relationships within the neighborhood and is the place where those relationships are daily reaffirmed by the men present. Lastly, for those involved, it is a place for exchanging gossip, taking a cool drink and having fun.

Unlike the house and yard, where he feels himself to be subject to the regular constraints of family and neighbors, the streets represent a man's freedom. In a poorer neighborhood freedom is a relative concept and often one is without the means to undertake the most limited of expeditions. But, it is freedom in the sense that life on the streets is autonomy and provides one with the sense of being in control that is so important to the men who gather here regularly.

Beneath the overt manifestations of fraternity and good fellowship, mutual drinking, conversational camaraderie, non-threatening dispositions and verbal affirmations that all those present are true and honorable representatives of "manhood," there lies a covert suspicion that the others present, in some way and at some time will try to exploit you. And the feeling that when support — financial or moral — is desperately needed it will not be forthcoming from this group.

This theme is subtly expressed in the caution exercised in establishing new relationships and in assuring that established relationships are not extended too deeply. A request made and not fulfilled either because the one requested won't or can't comply, is an open statement that the group is not what it is meant to be. On a symbolic level this feeling is often expressed in the proverb (*odo*): "Friends are good but also friends are not good" (*Mati boen, ma mati no boen*).

Outside of the *winkel*, these men belong to no common membership groups. No clubs, associations, activities or other points and places of congregation draw these men, in part or entirely, into a larger more inclusive unit. Outside of the

TABLE I
WINKEL CREW BY AGE, SALARY, RESIDENCE, MATING ARRANGEMENT.

Name	Age	Education	Monthly Salary	Skilled/ Unskilled	Residence	Location	Mating Present	Mating Past
Marcell	24	Elementary	Sf 380	Skilled	Paternal aunt and concubine	Frimangron	Concubinage	Visiting
Schill	53	High School	Sf 500	Skilled	Alone	One mile from Frimangron	Visiting	Concubinage
Russel	55	Incomplete Elementary	Sf 210	Unskilled	Concubine	Frimangron	Concubinage	Visiting
Geld	48	Elementary	Sf 295	Semi-skilled	Alone	Frimangron	Visiting	Concubinage
Elder	65	Incomplete Elementary	Sf 185	Unskilled	Concubine	Frimangron	Concubinage	Visiting and concubinage
Charlie	38	Elementary	Sf 280	Skilled	Concubine	Frimangron	Concubinage	Visiting
Toriman	46	High School	Sf 290	Skilled	Concubine	Frimangron	Concubinage	Visiting and concubinage
van Kamten	38	Two year College	Sf 500	Skilled	Concubine	Frimangron	Concubine	Visiting and married
Rijker	43	Middle School	Sf 350	Semi-skilled	Wife	Frimangron	Married	Visiting
Chris	28	Elementary	Sf 200	Unskilled	Concubine	Frimangron	Concubinage	Visiting
Bunker	36	Middle School	Sf 300	Skilled	Concubine	Frimangron	Concubinage	Visiting
Richard	24	Elementary	Sf 285	Unskilled	Maternal aunt	Frimangron	Visiting	Concubinage
Frankie	27	Elementary	Sf 240	Unskilled	Mother	Frimangron	Visiting	Visiting
Willem	42	Elementary	Sf 280	Unskilled	Alone	Frimangron	Visiting	Visiting
Jules	39	Elementary	Sf 310	Semi-skilled		Frimangron	Visiting	Visiting and concubinage
Tony	41	Incomplete	Sf 220	Unskilled	Concubine	Frimangron	Concubinage	Visiting

winkel, these men are not dependent on one another, nor do they even travel together except for two or three close friends.

If the men in the *winkel* are related to each other genealogically, the ties are so distant that no one recognizes them. If one investigates kinship relations between an ad hoc gathering of Creoles, some will have a common distant genealogical connection with some others. The small population, the tendency for lower-status Creoles to mate amongst themselves, a flexible mating system allowing for more than one mate and a far-flung web of cognatic descent combined with a broad ranging definition of personal kindred allow for this. In the *winkel* there are no rights and responsibilities of kinship expressed between any of the 15 men in any context.

This is all the more remarkable because for men and women — more so for the latter — discussions of family and kinship matters are daily conversational fare. And the men know who is in their family and kin group to quite a degree (see Pierce, 1971). A story often told at the *winkel* is that you must always tell your sons the names of the daughters you made with other women (the son's half-sisters) for fear of him someday accidentally mating with them and engaging in the "horror" of incest. So done, all sorts of supernatural tragedies will befall the unsuspecting parties (see Herskovits and Herskovits, 1936). Fictive kinship terms such as "my brother" are only rarely used.

The men belong to no clubs together. As far as membership in formal clubs (with recruitment policies, insignias defining restricted membership, scheduled meetings, and structured and enduring responsibilities between members), only those men who are upwardly mobile (or who wish their offspring to be upwardly mobile) are involved.

Mr. Rijker and his wife belong to the Order of Mechanics, the least prestigious, but yet important, secret lodge in Paramaribo. It draws in members principally from the middle class. It is she who, like most women, is the most enthusiastic club member and she is the one who continually reminds her husband when and where the meetings are. They dress up to attend the monthly gatherings, she in a lively print dress topped by a straight haired wig and straw hat — no plaited hair here — he in a dark suit. Mr. Rijker is the only man in the *winkel* who owns a suit.

Apart from regular appearances at meetings the lodge requires the regular remittance of dues and attendance at events both scheduled and unanticipated — fund-raising parties, wakes for deceased members, initiation meetings and so forth. Lodge obligations are "more" than most *winkel* men care for and they see no point in joining such an organization, or the others — Masons, Odd Fellows, etc. — like it.

Schill on the other hand, enjoys club "high life." From his occasional visitations to the drinking bars, restaurants and casinos of downtown as well as a few brief trips to the Netherlands, Schill has developed a taste for bright lights, disco music and things "*modo*" (in the mode). He is a member of a private bar and occasionally takes one of his higher status girl friends there. He never takes a woman from the neighborhood for, as he says "they just would not know how to act." He gladly pays the membership fee of 250 guilders per year, because of the higher social position he aspires to and the possible favors he might later receive or bestow.

Schill can fit in, as his Dutch is fluent, he can talk with ease about national and international topics and he knows how the better groomed higher-ups behave. The fellows at the *winkel* — bellicose, loud, rambunctious and participating in the pleasures with every sense the mind and body can muster — feel constrained, uncomfortable, and quite bored with what they perceive as the impersonal, alien, stuffy and arrogant ambience of the downtown places. Though some of the men could afford it, none but Rijker and Schill belong to formal voluntary associations.

Political parties in Suriname are based largely on ethnic blocks (except those few small parties that may espouse a special ideological platform). By virtue of their ethnicity and socio-economic position all the men in the *winkel* either belong to or vote for the largest Creole party in Suriname. The platform of the NPS (*Nationale Partij Suriname*) has traditionally posed as the champion of the lower-status *nengre*. In fact, "Jopie" Pengel, the last NPS Prime Minister was a black man of modest origins and son of a school teacher. When the word goes out from party headquarters to mobilize for in activity or goal, it is the neighborhood women who do the organizing and who use common political participation and sentiment as a basis for incorporating (Brana-Shute, R., 1976). For the men, this political participation is a very individual commitment and in no way bundles the men together into an identifiable group where the men feel a common bond between themselves. Election day finds each man going his own separate way to the polls, or staying home, or sitting at the *winkel*. Save for Schill, none of the *winkel* crew are involved in a voluntary capacity for their party. Politics does not act as an integrating factor between men in the *winkel*-forum.

The men do not work together. No two individuals are employed at a common place. They do not depend on one another for transportation, assistance or advice. Unless somehow involved in neighborhood gossip, the men at the *winkel* never talk about the fellows with whom they work nor do they visit them or invite them to the *winkel*. These men have their own *winkels* in their own neighborhoods and, unless a strong friendship develops, the workplace does not draw men together in instrumental relationships. Trade unions are widespread in Suriname but, like membership in party politics, they have little bearing on the daily conduct of the men's neighborhood lives.

Although most of the *winkel* regulars had lived or do live in the same neighborhood, their work carries them to commercial downtown Paramaribo and, for some, into different parts of Suriname. The men do not reside together. In the first place, this would be grounds for suspicion of homosexuality. There is really no need for the men to reside together as it would neither simplify the division of household labor nor greatly reduce the monthly rent. Houses are inexpensive for these men, and food, laundry, mending, sex and so forth are taken care of by groups of women who are located in their own households.

The men do not rotate or share women among themselves. Competition for women is keen although not hostile, but when two men who know each other are involved sexually with the same women it can only lead to trouble. A *winkel* man will go to great lengths to avoid even encountering another's woman. A conversation with her could seriously suggest that you had designs. The men rarely take women out for a stroll, to a movie, for a drink, to church. All visitation takes place within the confines of a house. "Could you imagine," they say, "if you took your woman out and one of your other women saw you." Even if a scene were avoided at the time of contact, there would certainly be hostility at the next meeting. Men avoid places where women congregate; the encounter of two lovers in the presence of their common male has led to many a *kroetoe* (argument, verbal encounter) particularly at birthday parties, wakes and funerals.

Such public displays of outrage, which are avidly attended by and participated in by passersby, bring forth anger unmatched by the furies and possible shame and loss of "respect" to the parties concerned.

A misfortune of this type befell Frankie late one Sunday morning as he was leisurely passing a church on the way to the *winkel*. As luck would have it the congregation was leaving and two of his women, unknown to each other, simultaneously emerged. There was no place for him to escape. Recognizing their common interest the two females turned on each other and the combat was on. As the crowd gathered about the contestants — easily six deep — both women proceeded to heap scorn and humiliation on the adversary. Frankie slipped away.

One woman got the better of the contest through her superior knowledge of the other's genealogy and foibles. Reciting past scandals she closed by pointing out that her opponent could never hope to sexually satsify a man and, in fact, her vagina was infested with cockroaches. The crowd roared its approval and the victor marched away with coup counted and respect tarnished, but intact. The vanquished one refused to talk with Frankie ever again and so upset was she that she later solicited the services of an obeah man to help her re-establish spiritual equilibrium. (For traditional Surinamers closely attuned to their Afro-slave heritage, social conflict often results in severe psychological trauma that can only be expiated by ritual therapy. More of this in Chapter IV.)

There are certain safeguards to assure that men in the *winkel* have no contact with one another's woman or women. If one needs to contact a fellow crew member, one goes to the *winkel* and spreads the word. It is best left to Chung, the proprietor for, as the respository of neighborhood messages, he knows the schedule of each of the men, their general wherabouts and is in contact with people who have contact with the individual so sought. One rarely goes directly to a man's residence to seek him; (aside from his probably not being there) this would suggest baiting his woman. Even if the man is at home, say the men, she will not tell you of his whereabouts anyway. She would not want you to draw him out of the house to spend more money or make more contacts with other women.

There is no common participation in extra-*winkel* activities. During the wide spread strikes of early 1973 there was a great deal of activity in downtown Paramaribo. Union meetings were held, politicians gave addresses and held meetings, ceremonies were held for fallen comrades, and people gathered to watch police-protestor encounters and the subsequent violence. At no time did the men leave the *winkel* to watch, attend, or engage in the phenomena with someone else from the *winkel*. Daily, after their independent excursions to a point of interest, each would return to the corner and the events would be debated with relish.

The nature of these male groups in Paramaribo stands in contrast to those explored by Wilson (1974) on the island of Providencia. Concerning the cohesiveness of the Providencia groups he states (1974: 158): "In an almost spontaneous, accidental way the men of a community divide up into small groups of approximately four to seven members. They are essentially groups of equals — of the same generation if not the same age, of the same life situation, and with a mutual compatibility." The *winkel* "crews" of Paramaribo appear a good deal more diffuse than those of Providencia, as Wilson (1974: 173) goes on to point out: "Socially, then, membership in a crew also implies an entree into a ramifying network of ties which, if the circumstances called for it, could be politically advantageous too." It is doubtful that a Paramaribo crew could be converted into an instrumental, goal-committed, semi-corporate interest group.

The only time a portion of these men act in concert is when there is a party or ritual to which some of them are entitled to attend. However, this does not draw the men together as a group, but merely calls together eligible individuals located in a common point. This is in no way a cooperative effort, for the men are unrelated among themselves. They are not considered a "group apart" by the initiator of the call and all maintain different relationships with the "caller." Only those men from the *winkel* who are invited attend the function. Should two, three or all of the men belong to a common other's network they will attend but their motives for going together are not generated by any intra-*winkel* motives or bonds. Their behavior as a group is externally imposed.

The *winkel* men establish their most important and elaborate extra-*winkel* ties with their respective household groups. If these relationships were studied by employing females and children as the point of investigation this realization would not emerge so forcefully. However, when the focus is on the male, it becomes obvious that households are crucial to him, although he is absent, and that he is simultaneously very important to several dispersed clusters of women.

These men are temporary and part-time members of all the households and residences, either consanguineal or conjugal, with which they have contact. Because of the extensive exchange networks radiating out from each male, they cannot become committed full-time to any one residential cluster and as a result become marginal to all in which they participate. As well as being fathers and lovers to a number of children and mothers, they are also sons and brothers to other women. In a lower-class situation where wide and varied support networks of individuals are preferred over the consolidation of resources in one domestic group, specific households are embedded in networks radiating from male brokers strategic to socio-economic success and striving. Household maintenance taps these men, as well as a localized kindred, as multiple conjugal ties and consanguines are manipulated. The social contacts so formed act as channels conveying goods and services in many directions, ultimately mitigating against the consolidation of resources in any one group.

In a sexual partnership system that sanctions visiting and concubinage, and marriage at an older age, any number of contacts with women, resulting in children, can be made. All of these contacts require some financial contribution and siphon off aid that could have been made available to the man's current or future household. Indeed, local definition of manhood has it that men should have both a number of children and support them. Consorting with many young women hardly blemishes a man's reputation in the eyes of other men. In addition to lovers, it is widely acknowledged that a man must contribute financially to the maintenance of his mother.

Unless a male is able to make a large contribution to a woman, and keep her from complaining about wages being siphoned off to other households, his position with her is not secure. Should he not adequately maintain the household of his woman, he forces her to seek financial assistance from other sources: a job (if possible), gifts from relatives, or other men, who in turn, may or may not be present in her household.

When a male begins a visiting relationship with a woman he is careful to note if she has children or not. If he lives with her in concubinage he is not legally responsible to support either her or her children. However, the woman has an excellent bargaining point in her children and may well point out that the children, although not his, have to be supported and that he is the household "breadwinner." He can take it or leave it.

The woman may also press the male to legally recognize the children as his own (if the genitor has not already done so). If a male chooses this alternative — few men do — he must accept full financial responsibility for the children as set down by national legal standards. It is not surprising, that with such a rigorous outcome possibly resulting from a simple mating relationship, few men establish long term relationships with women who have "unrecognized children" and opt for the more tenuous visiting relationship.

In contrast, children function as a survival strategy for women. It is widely acknowledged that children are a form of "life insurance" in old age. However, during the younger years, even though they are a burden and have to be supported, they also serve to maintain a woman's contact with a number of men, and assure that money enters the household. Radcliffe-Brown's (1950: 49) assertion that children are the final consummation of a marriage applies as well, in an on-going financial sense, for visiting and concubinage relationships.

Outside the *winkel* these men run their lives independently of one another. What then throws them together? The *winkel* is a common accessible point in space where men in a similar domestic situation can gather. They are "half-way" between households because they have refused to commit themselves to any one. Marginal to all the households in which they participate, the men, in many ways, have no place else to go. However, I would not describe the social function of the *winkel* quite as strongly as Liebow does in speaking of a Washington, D.C. Afro-American streetcorner where:

> In self-defense, the husband retreats to the streetcorner. Here, where the measure of man is considerably smaller, and where the weaknesses are somehow turned upside down and almost magically transformed into strengths, he can be, once again, a man among men. (1967: 136)

The fellows who gather regularly at the *winkel* are not "crushed and defeated," looking at society through the prism of "disorganization" but, rather, are holding on to what they have and what they think they can get in an environment that asks little else from them. Paramaribo shops are not the desperate haunts of the "damned of the earth," but congregation points for males in the particular social organization in which they participate.

In the neighborhood of *Frimangron* and others like it in Paramaribo, the street corner is the natural focus of displays of manly character. Young men, after they have left school drift quite easily to the corner and begin to experiment with the roles and identities encountered there. They learn not only about leisure but about its value. They also learn the importance of being an individual, a "somebody" accepted and admired by their peers, yet sufficiently outstanding in terms of some personal attribute to be recognized as unique.

In one way or another these concerns all involve a man's reputation and the importance of establishing a presence in the world. A reputation has many facets; to father children is a sign of strength in the sense of character and spirit. And, as Wilson (1973: 150) writes, "this sense of a man's strength is the foundation of his reputation, that constellation of qualities by which he achieves a place in the world of others where he is both an equal and unique person. A man's reputation is the stimulus of other people's respect for him, and a concern for respect, for one's good name, is always smoldering ... reputation stipulates the minimum requirements for adult manhood and respect."

Reputations are earned and involve the acquisition of a battery of other skills. He must learn how to argue, tell stories, drink and perform real or imagined feats of spiritual and physical strength. Such activities lead to an informal ranking of men on the basis of reputation. (They also lead to a negation of the man's character by "outsiders"; school teachers, police, social workers, churchmen, officialdom and those of loftier position.) Finally, there is knowledge, the kind that is based on experience (*ondrofeni*). Knowledge, too, leads to reputation, and so it is important to have a variety of experiences of the world upon which to draw.

In this group setting a special sense of time, unbridled by clocks and work schedules develops. One's place in time becomes firmly situated in the present, the physical. The day, that gathering of friends, is to be experienced and consumed. The rhythm would later continue — at some unforeseen, but expected time — and, persons acting out their own time-tables would again appear and partake of self and others. The men, lounging, chatting, arguing or staring are not waiting for something to happen, it is happening and a person perceives himself as one who gives shape and meaning to time, and not as one who is merely a passive spectator awaiting the next round of scheduled activities.

The overwhelming group socialization patterns of lower-class men are expressions of their situation, and as such they provide a means whereby boys, and later men, achieve a satisfaction in confirming their own identity in a common culture and building up a sense of solidarity based on common values and sentiment. The *winkel* is a very special place.

Chapter three — Off the Corner

If joe pina wan oema a go teki tra man (If you deny a woman she will take another man).
A Surinamese proverb

The *winkel* is an enjoyable place to be. The men are mutually supportive by their very presence and their common symbolic behavior. Reputation is built and perpetuated here.

Men are most easily located singly or in groups at the *winkel*. However, their more important "survival" relationships are with other people in other places. These are relationships with a number of female consanguines and conjugals residing in many households. The men, although removed in space and in infrequent and sometimes non-recurrent contact with these households, participate in crucial reciprocal exchange arrangements vital to household maintainance.

Out of the fifteen or so men who gather at the *winkel*, not one participates in the family, household or residential affairs of any of the other men. When day is done they return separately to other places independently of one another. There is no cooperation after the day's activities at the *winkel*. Here the importance of women is thrown into sharp relief.

Winkel behavior and household behavior are not mutually exclusive for males. There is a great deal of overlap and what goes on in one arena replicates, complements and reinforces what goes on in the other. The *winkel* is a social shock absorber that mediates disturbances in the system. Two important adjustments relating to sex roles are carried out in the *winkel* context: 1) the solidifying of male social relationships (both dyads and networks) through mutual support, and 2) actual household rearrangement as men react to changes in their domestic situations.

Throughout their lives males form a series of contacts with women. In their childhood and youth household and domestic relationships are usually with clusters of consanguineally related women. Adolescent and adult years lead to sexual experimentation and conjugal activity, suggesting a developmental mating cycle from early extra-residential mating, through concubinage and faithful concubinage to, perhaps, marriage. However, this process is not always a linear time march of events. In short, extra-residential mating does not necessarily process into concubinage; the possibilities are many and simultaneous.

The following describes some common varieties of household-domestic relationships of the adult wage-earning males in the *winkel*. When, where and with whom do these men join when they establish domestic relationships? The process of recruitment of males into household clusters, the contacts they activate, deactivate and reactivate over time indicates that women related as uterines stay together in one spot or, if separated, maintain very close and intense ties (Pierce, 1971). On the other hand, men as consanguines or temporary conjugals, appear and reappear in marginal, sometimes extra-residential, relationships.

Household-Winkel Interaction

The household and *winkel* are sedentary points in space in a temporal field of shifting social relationships. There are, however, regular reappearing types of arrangements that tie the *winkel* to dispersed households and households to other households. The urban lower-class family, household, and domestic group may be visualized as a social field of changing social relationships spanning many households, linked together at points of regular male congregation. It is these male points of congregation — *winkels* — that function to re-establish balance in a field of exchange and maintainance networks often punctuated by changes of personnel or the modification of their relationships.

Following Chapple and Coon (1942: 418) the *winkel* could be considered as a form of association: A group of people (men) who have established the same type of relationship with others (women) and with each other (marginal males) and have begun to interact regularly on that basis. The mens' *winkel* participation is a function of their household situation. When there is a shock in the household it is absorbed in the *winkel*. The *winkel* as association allows the men to make adjustments to disturbances in other institutions (e.g., change in household membership, loss of a job, etc.) by allowing compensatory interaction in a neutral area.

Genealogically, kinship ties males economically to a number of households. By birth a male gains membership in a bilateral kindred distributed over space.[21] The kindred is not localized nor is it bounded or corporate. However, a male can strategically activate these geneological ties for purposes of establishing a support network (occasional residence, domestic services, inheritance rights and privileges).

Reciprocal support is provided most usually through his female consanguines. It is quite normal, for instance, for a male at the termination of a concubinage relationship to reside temporarily at the home of one of his female consanguines and to temporarily become a vital member in that domestic group.

Rules of descent and inheritance complement ego's membership in a kindred. Movable property and real estate are passed on bilaterally to off-spring. With parents dying intestate all full siblings, recognized legally by the father, receive equal shares of the patrimony. Children automatically inherit from their mothers. Half-siblings of the same mother are not functionally distinguished; the only difference is that they would, if recognized by the father (*erkennen*), inherit property from different fathers. Real estate, traditionally, is impartible and the result is "sibling land" (Clarke, 1957) with each sibling gaining the right to live on and exploit the plot of ground. Informal negotiations usually result in the sibling without house or land of his or her own assuming control of the deceased parent's (or parents') property. The right usually devolves upon females who tend to remain with their mothers after a series of extra-residential, concubinal relationships. They in turn maintain the households to which their brothers may return. Absent siblings are not denied their traditional rights of exploiting a plot of ground. Should a will have been drawn up then its stipulations are followed. Wills, however, are only infrequently drawn up.

Usually, when the male is an adult wage earner, he leaves his consanguineal household to establish a household with a concubine while perhaps maintaining a number of extra-residential mates as well. The possibilities are many; he may return frequently to his consanguineal household for material service, return only occasionally to make remittances or he may virtually ignore his consanguineal household. The latter alternative is considered heinous by lower-class Creoles who feel it is a moral responsibility for a man to contribute to his mother's upkeep.

If the male has inherited nothing and his consanguines live on rented land his return to them is less sure. He must have something substantial to contribute to the household. Although children are expected to support their parents, the link between a man and his children may be tenuous, especially if the man has engaged in a number of mating relationships with different women throughout his life.

Extra-residential mating and concubinage tie a man affinally and consanguineally to a large number of households. If such a relationship is physically terminated the male is still responsible by law to provide support for the children he made with different mothers. Child support is endorsed by the government and, until the child's maturity, a man is responsible to make remittances to the households where his progeny reside. It is not expected that these households provide residential services for the male. A sensitive point between a man and his current woman is that sometimes a substantial portion of his income is siphoned off from her household to provide support for another.

Mating relationships persist with some tenacity although the physical contact between males and females may be infrequent and irregular. Although the male is required to support only the children, he may regularly make remittances to the woman if he chooses to maintain the relationship as potentially activatable. The relationships may then lie dormant, only to become reestablished when it suits one or the other's strategies.

A mating system, which sanctions multiple and simultaneous extra-residential mating, visiting, concubinage, and marriage within the context of a bilateral kinships system results in each ego, male or female, being surrounded by a network of ex-mates with whom children may or may not have been produced. The kindred and descent group becomes broadened as spouses, lovers, fathers, mothers, children, siblings, half siblings, etc. leave home and reside in dispersed households. Capital, goods and services regularly flow into and between households along these lines from non-household residents.[22]

Birthdays are the most important recurrent life cycle rites. Every fifth celebration (*bigi jari*) for an adult Creole calls for a lavish expenditure of time and money to organize and expedite a party drawing together dispersed kindred and portions of the cognatic descent group.[23] Although prior contact may have been minimal, males attend the gatherings.

Wakes function in the same capacity. As a member of many overlapping cognatic descent groups (a person is a member of as many cognatic descent groups as he has apical ancestors) a male is genealogically tied to a large number of living and dead ancestors. Under these genealogical circumstances, and in daily practice, it is impossible to include ego in any sort of permanent, corporate, ancestor focused descent group. However, the death of a cognate identifies a bounded group of descendants of the deceased and, for the purposes of executing the ritual, brings into being a temporarily identifiable group of co-descendants. The mechanism that identifies this group is not an internal rule of kinship itself, but an extra-kinship action that triggers the definition of a temporary, bounded descent group. Ego's participation may be negligible or intense. With the execution and end of the ceremony, this sub-cognatic descent group dissolves back into the larger on-going descent group (Brana-Shute and Brana-Shute, 1977).

Ritual assemblage for the purpose of executing the *winti* (spirit) cult dances and ceremonies draws males into contact with larger groups of relatives some of whom may be useful to him. An individual or a family can sponsor a *winti pre* (spirit play) for the purpose of providing individual or group therapy.[24] Spirits, which are inherited bilaterally through the descent groups, are present during these carefully orchestrated congregations and states of possession. Males attend these rites and are spiritually and socially reunited with their relatives, ancestors and deities in a brief, but intense, ritual or series of rituals. Through the ritual schedule of birthdays, wakes, and spirit dances it may be incumbent upon the male to donate goods, services and /or capital. For lower-class Creole males who have marginal and shifting relationships (or at least the lack of total commitment) to their affinal households, most of their ritual resources are allocated to consanguines.

Child loaning or fosterage (*kwetchi pikin*) is a widespread phenomenon among Creoles and acts as a transgenerational link between dispersed households. Although this does not articulate the *winkel* directly with households, it does serve to establish links between groups of women who may place the temporary care of one of their children in the hands of another household.

Clubs and voluntary associations are women's fare and act as channels drawing females and female-headed households into contact with one another. These organizations have rules, recruitment policies, ensignias, symbols, meeting places, scheduled activities and multifaceted functions. Creole Suriname is not devoid of organizations beyond the household, nor are lower-class women limited in their movement to house, hearth and market.

The clubs provide instrumental services aside from what their fancy titles would presuppose. At the completion of a club meeting, the relationships do not dissolve until the next meeting, but remain, keeping clusters of active women in contact with one another (Brana-Shute, R., 1976).

Dynamic links serve to articulate the *winkel* and households with each other. For the male, the most instrumental of these are his consanguineal kinship networks and his mating relationships with a number of woman. Networks of economic exchange and support, temporary residence, satisfaction of domestic services, access to property, and mechanisms for ritual assemblage are embedded in the relationships. However, to fully grasp the nature of the relationships and their content, they must be viewed over time as the process of activating, deactivating and reactivating of these social contacts unfolds in an environment of *winkel,* household and neighborhood.

What does go on in the household affects *winkel* behavior and vice versa. The men are marginal to their households, and the nature of the relationships they form with women is subject to frequent disturbances: departures, reentries, quarrels, animosities. The men need to interact with other men to compensate for disturbances in the households in which they had interacted and do so along male channels already in existence.

Four short tales follow. They are intended to illuminate how men and women manipulate their dyadic contacts within the context of family and household, kith and kin. Two of them deal with young men — Jules and Marcell — and the living arrangements these men have made for themselves. I have included Betty's story — the woman of hapless Russel — to demonstrate the adaptations females make when sharing a man with other women and the *winkel*. The story of old Rudolf also follows, a man past his prime, unwanted by consanguines and conjugals alike.

A Few Tales

Jules

Every night, if he is not visiting a woman or leading the singing at an all night wake, Jules returns alone to his house, a two room cottage. Morning finds him on his way to work.

Jules, at 38, is a likable fellow and most of the people in the neighborhood know him and enjoy his company. He has a number of women with whom he has relations, and his presence is always welcomed by the *winkel* crew.

Without following Jules' movements closely it would appear that he lives in a "single person household;" but Jules, as well as most men who live alone, relies on a group of people for domestic services spread wider than the residential parameters of his cottage.

Jules and John were born in the same neighborhood and became inseparable friends. They both got jobs at the aluminum company and brought home handsome salaries. Jules, however, was distracted by his singing chores which he clearly loved, and would often show up late or not at all for work. He was soon discharged while John remained on.

Eight years ago John began living with Henrietta. They have produced two children. A house and yard were bought (in John's name) and they live happily there. John does not frequent the *winkel*, preferring rather to invest surplus time and moneys into his home.

Anytime day or night (when Jules chooses not to attend the *winkel*) will find Jules sitting behind John's house talking, eating and drinking. After work John and Jules get together, pool some money and buy a quantity of beer. They sit until the late hours; Saturdays, Sundays, and holidays find the atmosphere more festive.

During the banter Henrietta serves meals; chicken, rice, vegetables, soups and bread. Jules can also stop by any time during the day and have a bite to eat. Henrietta also does Jules' washing and ironing and when Jules has need of a domestic service he is either unfamiliar with or chooses not to do he can call upon Henrietta. Except for sexual access, Henrietta provides virtually all household and domestic services for Jules.

Jules contributes to this "nuclear family household." Moneys are regularly given weekly to John and irregularly when extra food and drink must be provided for spontaneous or planned activities. Henrietta's birthday party found Jules doing most of the errands and organizing most of the activities (shopping, music arrangement, beer delivery, etc.). Jules, with his mechanical abilities, also does odd jobs around his host's house. He is forever fixing a motorcycle, iron, fence post or some other broken item, while John is at work. Sporadic gifts to the children and his own ability to inspire good fun fill out Jules' fare of contributions. He also helps in caring for the children; two young boys.

This relationship could convert probably into Jules' full time residence if need be. (Occasionally if he drinks too much and does not choose to ride his motorcycle home, Jules stays the night.) Jules is a very important member of this group, and without them his life would be considerably different. (The furnishings of Jules' house consist of nothing more than a frame bed and mattress; not even a hot plate stands in his kitchen.) He, at this point, chooses not to become involved with a woman on more than a visiting basis. He claims that such an arrangement would inhibit his widespread movements and involvement in activities.

It would at first appear that Jules, a man of streetcorner letters, lives alone in a "single person household." At least that is what the census documents would state. But Jules' domestic relationships span many households that provide him with services and, socially at least, his "house" is only one of many places he has to go.

Myra and Rudolf

Myra and Rudolf illustrate various processes in one example. At once we deal with a household whose real social boundaries are flung far over space. There is also, because of the untimely death of Myra, a series of intra-household realignments and transfer of property negotiations. Finally, there is the shedding of an older affinal male and his unplanned return to the streetcorner.

Myra is 64 years old and lives in a large yard in the center of *Frimangron*. Everyone in the neighborhood refers to the yard, Myra's house, the two other rented houses and the adjoining tailor shop and vegetable stand as "Myra's." However, it is more complicated than this. Myra, her sister and her deceased brother's four children rent out the two houses and the two enterprises located on this piece of family land and take yearly turns collecting the patrimony. This is how it came about.

In 1912 Myra's father lived on a small plot of ground outside Paramaribo. He wanted to move to the city to find salaried work and, with some accumulated capital, assumed a 75 year lease on a large plot of ground in a sparsely settled section of *Frimangron*. Under the provisions of the lease the land title could be renewed and rights to the property itself sold, mortgaged and legally inherited. Moving to the city in 1926, the father built three houses on the property. He rented two while he lived with his woman, his two daughters and son in the other. In 1956 he died and the land and its income passed as a unit to the three siblings who inherited equal shares. As Myra's parents were not married, neither the father's woman nor her relatives were beneficiaries. The old woman was allowed to live out her years, cared for, in a small back room.

Prior to the father's death, Myra's sister moved out to live with a man across town. The brother departed as well, leaving Myra, her second man, her five children and her mother and father on the property. All of Myra's siblings had rights to live on the land but only Myra chose to exercise them. Instead, after the death of the father each of the siblings received their capital share of the rent in turn once every three years.

In 1962, a tailor offered to buy a piece of the property. Myra, her sister and brother decided against selling but agreed to rent a plot to the businessman. Shortly thereafter the same procedure was followed with a vegetable vendor. The yearly rent grew. At this time the people living with Myra on the land were her third man Rudolf, her daughter Ester, Ester's daughter, and one of Myra's grandchildren (a daughter of one of Myra's deceased daughters).

In 1965 Myra's brother died, leaving two sons and a daughter. They assumed their father's legal inheritance rights, every three years getting their father's share of the rent and dividing it among themselves. Someday it will be further partitioned when it passes to their children. Satisfied in the assurance that they may collect the rent revenues, neither of them exercise the right to live or build on the property.

Myra took Rudolf, her third man, in 1965 when she was 56 years old. He moved in with Myra, her daughter, and granddaughter. He lived with them for three years, until he turned 65 and retired as a repairman in government service. Myra was an enterprising woman and hit upon a plan. Since Rudolf was in perfect health and as fit as any man 30 years his junior and, since vegetable prices were rising rapidly, it was decided to rent a piece of land in one of the rural districts to grow and sell greens. It would take a large capital investment to build a shelter, buy tools, fertilizer, seed, striplings and provisions, but Myra could muster necessary cash. Rudolf was dispatched to the rural plot.

Thereafter, any weekday morning found Myra at home with Ester and the children. Three afternoons a week she took the 45 minute bus ride and walked 4 kilometers down a side road to their plot (*boiti*) to help Rudolf in the fields, cook something special for him, assist in making charcoal and bring goods back to the city. This continued until Myra fell ill; at that point she went once a week only to pick up vegetables for sale and personal consumption in the city.

Saturdays found Rudolf in the city, sleeping and eating at Myra's house and enjoying the company of her grandchild whom he dearly loved. The household was well provisioned with cassava, beans, oranges, sugar cane, bananas, eggplants, charcoal and a myriad of local vegetables (plus herbs gathered on the property for use in medicinals), all grown on the *boiti*. Everyone in the neighborhood knew Myra had these items for sale and would stop by for fresh, quality goods at fair prices. The transaction was lubricated by friendship.

Rudolf is no longer a *winkel* habitué. Indeed, in his younger days he enjoyed the company of his fellow drinkers, but many had died or become infirm. He himself was no longer making an adequate salary to support these pastimes, and he wanted to settle down and spend time with his woman, her grandchild and gardens. Although he lost interest in the *winkel*, he would regularly stop in on Saturdays for a shot or two of rum. He is treated courteously by the *winkel* group as most older men are, but the relationship went no further.

When Myra died unexpectedly her funeral called together people from Paramaribo, the rural districts and even Holland. Myra was a traditional woman and the services did her justice. Eight days of night-long song and story-telling followed her death, and on the day of her funeral her sons carried her coffin around the yard for a last goodbye. Myra went to the grave ushered by flowers and trumpets.

Myra's sons paid for the funeral costs not covered by her burial society (*fonsoe*). Rudolf had a little money which he used to buy flowers for the coffin and the wake. In any case he was not expected to assume the responsibility. This was a family matter.

The inheritance was also a family matter. Myra's share of the rent revenues passed to her three sons and daughter. The brothers decided that, as they owned their own houses, Ester should be given the house and all its contents. They recognized that she was without a man to support her, without a job and with another child on the way. This arrangement was agreed to by Myra's living sister and the children of Myra's deceased brother. In the future, Myra's tri-yearly turn to the revenues would go to Myra's four children, who would share it equally. Rudolf, Myra's man, had no inheritance rights.

It was through the good will of Ester and her brothers that Rudolf would continue visiting the house in the city. Showing up less frequently, he stayed only long enough to shower kisses and sweets on the grandchild. Rudolf was also permitted to stay on the *boiti* which had passed to Ester and her brothers. He was expected to pay them the rent and, with the remaining proceeds from sales, provision himself.

Myra's children were not interested in marketing vegetables and, without Myra's financial investments and marketing contacts, Rudolf's income dwindled until he could barely buy himself a package of tobacco or pay bus fare to the rural district. His only contact with the once happy household had been through Myra and now, after her death, he was being sloughed off. Myra's patrimony had supported him. Without her and her reserves he was reduced to a very marginal position.

Rudolf is unwanted by his children from his three prior women. He had left their mothers and had not supported them in their youth. There is no room at their houses for a man with whom they have had little contact. Not yet seventy, he is not eligible for old age welfare. Rudolf has no living consanguineal kin with whom he can affiliate.

A few months after Myra's death a young man moved into the house with Ester. Rudolf's presence became an unwanted imposition. He now spends most of his time at his rural gardens. Rudolf is seen occasionally hawking vegetables from a basket attached to the front of his bicycle. He is old and practically destitute, two characteristics that mitigate against enduring participation both in *winkel* and household affairs.

Betty and Russel

Betty and Russel live together. Russel's reputation and *winkel* behavior were described in Chapter III. Although he does not possess a reputation of distinction, he spends most of his time and money at the *winkel*. In his absence Betty must make adjustments and engage in extra-household activities in order to maintain an adequate standard of living. Russel's household contacts are infrequent and attenuated.

On the face of it, Betty is dependent on her man Russel for support. Every month he gives her Sf 57 (a small sum even by conservative *winkel* standards) to pay household expenses, feed him and care for her aged and infirm mother. All Russel's domestic needs are cared for by Betty. Aside from remittances he, occasionally and with great prodding, does "man's work" around the house; painting, replacing a floor board, knocking fruit from trees with a heavy pole, and so forth.

If Betty were asked to fill out an income form she would dutifully note the Sf 57 from Russel and Sf 26.50 a month given her by the government for the mother's old age welfare. Betty, however, has grappled with her marginal position and developed strategies to survive. Though Betty complains of high prices and wastes nothing in her house — from the claws of chickens to bits and pieces of hoarded bloth — she is well fed and appears happy. Occupational multiplicity couched in a network of kinship and friendship is the earmark of Betty's relative success.

There is a tiny spare room in Betty's cottage. This she rents out to a boarder for Sf 5 a month. His rent payments are carefully recorded in a tattered notebook, noting that Sf 2 must go to pay for her life insurance policy while the other three will be put in a bank account for a "rainy day" or new material acquisition.

From her man's yard she collects olives and, pickling them, sells them by the jar (which are given her by friends) outside her house. Canipa and bread fruit from her back yard, as well as bananas, oranges and other local fruit given her by kinfolk in the districts are for sale as well. Betty is not a full-time vendor by any means, but her part-time sales conducted from a street front window bring in a tidy profit that may amount to Sf 30 in a good month.

Ironing occasionally comes in from a middle class family in an adjoining neighborhood. This is irregular and occurs only when the client is preoccupied with other things. Betty can capitalize on this and in her spare time earn Sf 15 or Sf 20 a month. The sporadic nature of the work actually fits nicely with Betty's strategies. If she were tied down with a full-time ironing job she would be denied the time and opportunity to pursue her other chores.

A quiet conversation in her sitting room is often interrupted by the clamor of children outside her window. They yell in demanding "ices" and Betty takes a tray of ice cubes from her refrigerator and sells flavored cubes for one, two, or three cents each depending on the type of syrup added. Her homemade cookies and cakes are sold in the same manner. Neighbors who live without the convenience of an icebox can come buy a tray of cubes for five cents.

Visiting relatives from the districts and relatives of her first man, now deceased, visit Betty for the day and bring her gifts of vegetables, ground crops and fish. Betty will not have to buy these items and she sets aside the money saved in a small vase on a dusty shelf. It will be channeled in another direction at some future time. Surplus food, in turn, can be brought as gifts when Betty goes visiting.

When time permits and prices at the market are right Betty will buy fruits to stew and sell. She does not "hawk" but explains that everyone in the neighborhood knows she often has things for sale. Yesterday, when time and reserve capital permitted, she bought Sf 1.50 worth of fruits and, preparing them with sugar and spices, sold them. She calculated a net profit of Sf 3.50. This money will be set aside to supplement part of her rotating credit organization payment.

Even though Betty lives in an urban environment she gathers food. She knows of a tamarind tree on a busy intersection downtown. From the fruit of this tree she prepares a syrup consumed as a drink. In season she can be seen, in the middle of Paramaribo, gathering up the fallen fruits from the public tree.

This list could go on and on. Money flows in, in varying amounts and at erratic times, to her house and supports her and her mother at a standard of living unattainable if they had to rely completely on Russel's contributions. Betty carries all of this information around in her head and, like most Creole women, constantly mulls over strategies, prices, expenditures and possibilities for maximizing what resources she has at her disposal.

If Betty has income she also has heavy expenditures. She does not attack the supermarket armed with huge cart to haul home the week's groceries; her available capital does not permit such a regular expenditure. At the beginning of each month, however, she does take the past month's savings and lay in important stores. Betty could not get any credit at the fancy supermarkets of downtown where prices are cheaper but the neighborhood Chinese, who dispenses goods at a higher price from his corner *winkel*, will give her the credit she needs. Monthly she buys 50 pounds of rice, 5 pounds of margarine, a bucket of sugar, 3 liters of cooking oil, a 12 pound gas bomb for her stove and charcoal for her burner, most on credit.

If Betty could buy a box of 300 chicken boullion blocks, three or four of which she uses daily to flavor her sauces, she would. Limited funds do not permit such a lavish expenditure; to deplete all of one's resources at one time is foolhardy for it means not to consider the vicissitudes of tomorrow. As a result, Betty takes a daily stroll to the *winkel* and disburses ten cents for three blocks. This is a household chore, but it is also entertainent. In the course of her chore she will engage in playful banter, be privy to the latest gossip and pass on her messages (*boskopoe*).

In worrying about tomorrow Betty sets aside money for her and her mother's burial association (*fonsoe*), rotating credit organization (*kas moni*) and club (*vereniging*).

The burial association will pay for the costs of her funeral: casket, flowers, gravediggers and pall bearers. She also pays Sf 10 a month to her rotating credit association. It is run by an old woman in the neighborhood and most of the members know one another. Should one not pay in turn (thus upsetting the functioning of the cycle) the censure of the neighborhood would fall upon her. When Betty's turn comes up she receives Sf 250. The last time she was paid she bought a washing machine. The time before she carefully timed her turn to coincide with the week before her fiftieth birthday so she could buy alcohol, food, and all the other trappings for her party. Betty could also arrange a "loan" from her credit association more easily than from a commercial organization. Knowing all the women she could ask one of them to skip a turn and allow her to collect instead. No interest would be paid nor would strangers from downtown pry into her affairs.

Betty belongs to two clubs; one is a "pleasure club" and the members hold parties and dances, go to one another's birthdays and take bus excursions to the districts for outings. All members are female except for the President! From the monthly dues the members pay, each gets an envelop on her birthday containing Sf 25. A large bouquet of flowers is sent and some club sisters give a hand in the party cooking, serving and cleaning up. At death the club is there too.

Some might shake their heads in dismay over the expenditures Betty must make for her club. When a dance is held she completely outfits herself in new shoes, dress, pocketbook and head tie. Her gold is taken from its hiding place and so adorned Betty is a magnificent vision of womanhood, uplifting her spirit and the spirit of most observers (she makes quite a few people jealous too). If one follows Betty to the dance, one sees all the others attired in the same fabric, exhibiting a colorful display of solidarity.

Her club membership is an outgrowth of and embedded in other prior social relationships. Not only are the club members her co-sisters, but they are also her kinsmen, friends, neighbors and co-members in other organizations. In short, the relationships these women have with one another are many and complex, each one charged with intensity, durability and content.

When Betty has a problem that her limited and irregular resources cannot deal with she can call upon other women for help. Without them she would be in a plight and survival would not come easily. These clubs are not middle class Koffee Klatsches or ladies civic organizations; they are instrumental cooperative organizations, wherein a group of women band together to solve problems few of them could handle singly.

If Betty "lives only for today" and "seldom saves" it is only because her limited access to resources forces her to assume this behavior. She invests what little she has in local neighborhood organizations that will someday pay returns with social, psychological and capital dividends. If an observer notices only her new dress, her gay songs and lively dance steps, and muses over how frivolously lower class Creoles waste their money, then, sadly, he has missed the point (Figure Five).

Marcell

Marcell spends most of his free time at the *winkel*. There he has an impressive reputation. He has a well-paying, skilled, blue collar job, a large number of women whom he visits while he lives with one of them, and consumes great quantities of whiskey with his fellows without getting obnoxiously drunk or engaging in damaging gossip about other fellow members. To seek Marcell at one of his households is folly; he is with the men of the neighborhood.

However, operating from his *winkel* base, Marcell has had frequent relationships of varying duration with a number of households. The variety of contacts he forms are many; he regularly sleeps in some households, eats in others and with others his physical presence is not at all a prerequisite. A sporadic remittance may be his only contact with a household, a reminder of past services rendered or future services expected.

Marcell has been affiliated with a number of households throughout his life. Before adulthood and the development of his wage earning capacity, Marcell was dependent on consanguineàl households for nurture. As he matured sexually and financially, his relationships with households grew more shifting and complex. Mating and extra-residential relationships with women added a new dimension to his relationships and altered the frequency, intensity and duration of his older, yet still on-going, relationships. This story will explore the nature of Marcell's household contacts formed during his life. The numbers cited in this section refer to characters in the accompanying figures.

Marcell (1) was born twenty-nine years ago in a small cottage in *Frimangron*. Those living in the house at the time were Marcell's mother (2), Marcell's father (3), Marcell's mother's sister (4) and Marcell's brother Ferdie (5). This arrangement persisted until Marcell was three years old (Figure Six).

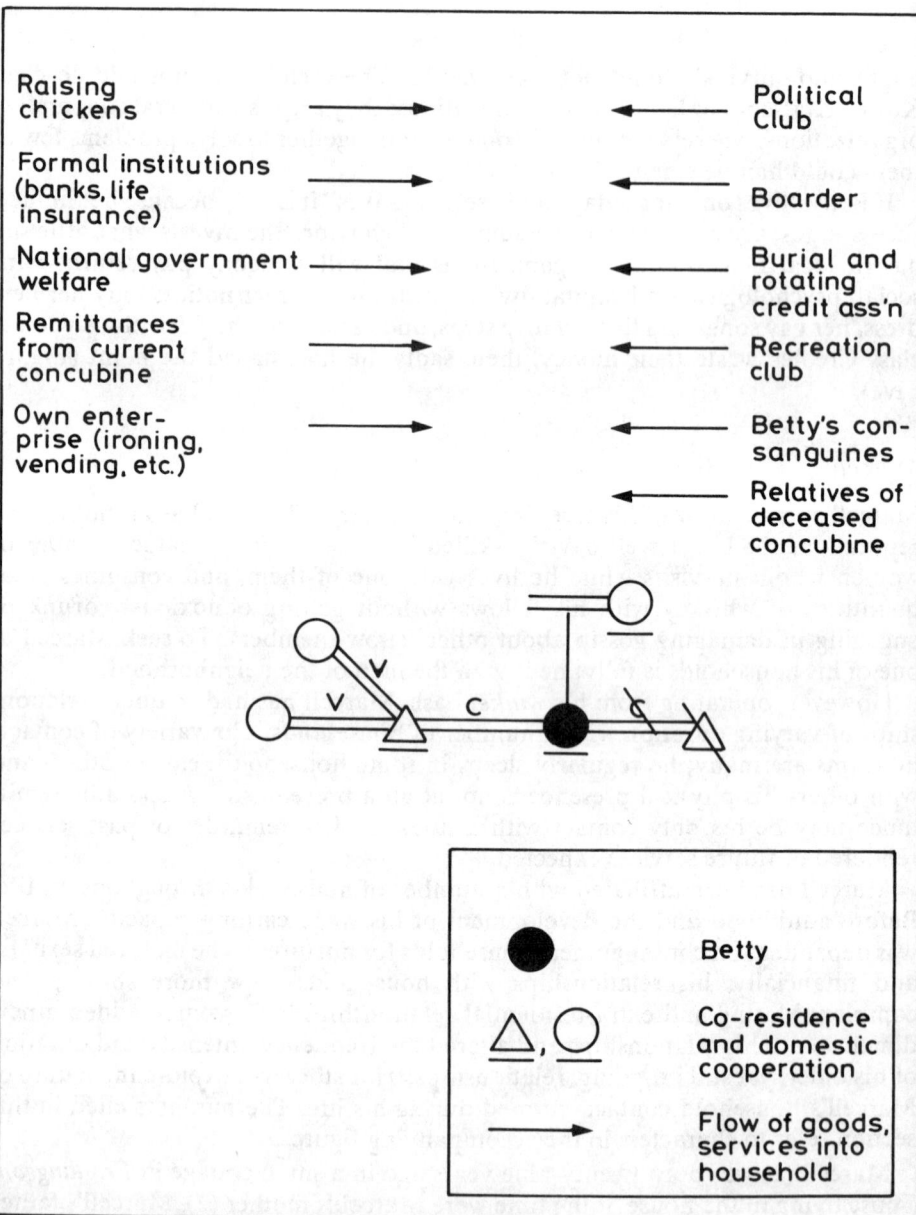

Figure five   Betty's household and tangent arrangements

The group moved to another house in the area and during the following two years underwent some organizational shifts in personnel. During this time his father (3) moved out and began living with Carol (6). In the father's absence Marcell's mother was visited by Tony (7) by whom she bore a son (8). While visiting with Tony she began living in concubinage with Bere (9) with whom she bore a daughter (10). Marcell's brother Ferdie resided with this group as well. The two years that Marcell resided with this group, when he was six and seven years old, were wrought with hardship and physical beatings. When the mother threw Bere out and took up with Boil (11), a rather callous man, Marcell was driven out and reestablished residence with his father and his woman a few streets away. Marcell's mother died shortly thereafter.

This residential arrangement also underwent a series of modifications. When Marcell was ten, he was joined by his brother Ferdie. The household, composed of Marcell, his brother, his father and his father's woman remained in this form until he was sixteen years old.

At that time the father and his woman argued and she left to live alone a few houses down the street. Six months later the father joined her. Marcell and his brother resided alone until Marcell turned eighteen when, again, he and his

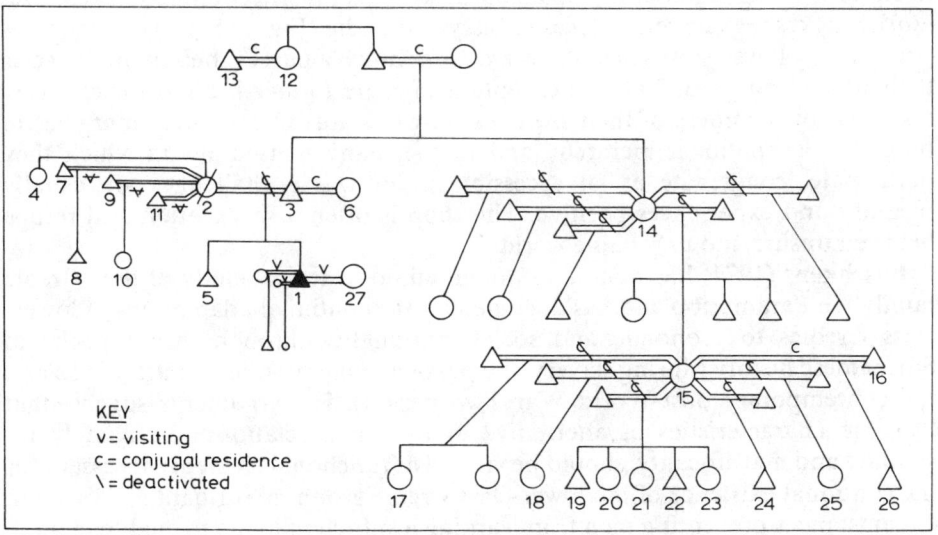

Figure six   Marcell's kin

brother were permitted to move in with his father and father's woman.

This arrangement lasted for about six months until Marcell and the woman had a series of fights. In anger she threw him out. The father said nothing. Marcell then moved in with his paternal great aunt (12) and her man. The woman was old and Marcell found living with the elderly couple difficult. He was young and his movements and activities did not easily mesh with those of his hosts. He left after a year.

Marcell then moved in with his paternal aunt Sissy (14), her daughter Sadie (15), Sadie's sixth man (16) and Sadie's ten resident children from six different fathers (17, 18, 19, 20, 21, 22, 23, 24, 25 and 26). This fourteen member group resided in two contiguous houses in a typical back yard arrangement. Each house has a downstairs cooking area and a sitting room (unused in the daytime and slept in at night) and an upstairs sleeping loft.

Marcell has lived off and on with this group for the last nine years. For a while he visited extra-residentially with a young Javanese woman (27). At the same time he regularly visited three other women and produced children with two of them. During this period Marcell's father moved and Marcell rented his house as a *dorose ose* (outside house) where he could take his women in privacy while still living at Sissy's. He kept his valuables at Sissy's as well as taking his meals there. Even now, living together (*libi makandra*) with his favorite woman in his *dorose oso*, he makes regular remittances to Sissy and Sadie (Figure Seven).

For many lower-status men the *winkel* is as much a part of their living space as their house and yard, with the exception that the former is almost exclusively reserved for members of their own sex. Lower-status Creole men, marginal to both the occupational hierarchy and to the many households in which they participate, congregate at an accessible point where challenges are usually pleasant and experiences positive. The shop is often a way station and refuge between unsure and unreliable worlds.

Buschkens (1974) has done a thorough ethno-historical study of the "Creole family" in Paramaribo and has documented the continual adaptations of lower-class Creoles to economic and social marginality through three epochs of Surinamese history (during slavery, the post-emancipation period after 1863 and the contemporary post-World War Two period). His arguments suggest that "... the characteristics of alternative man-woman relationships, namely instability and matrifocality, should be viewed as functional elements necessary for the continual existence of the lower-class Creole group in Surinam, ... living in circumstances preventing men from earning a sufficient living to enable them to support a household on a permanent basis." The organization of "family" and

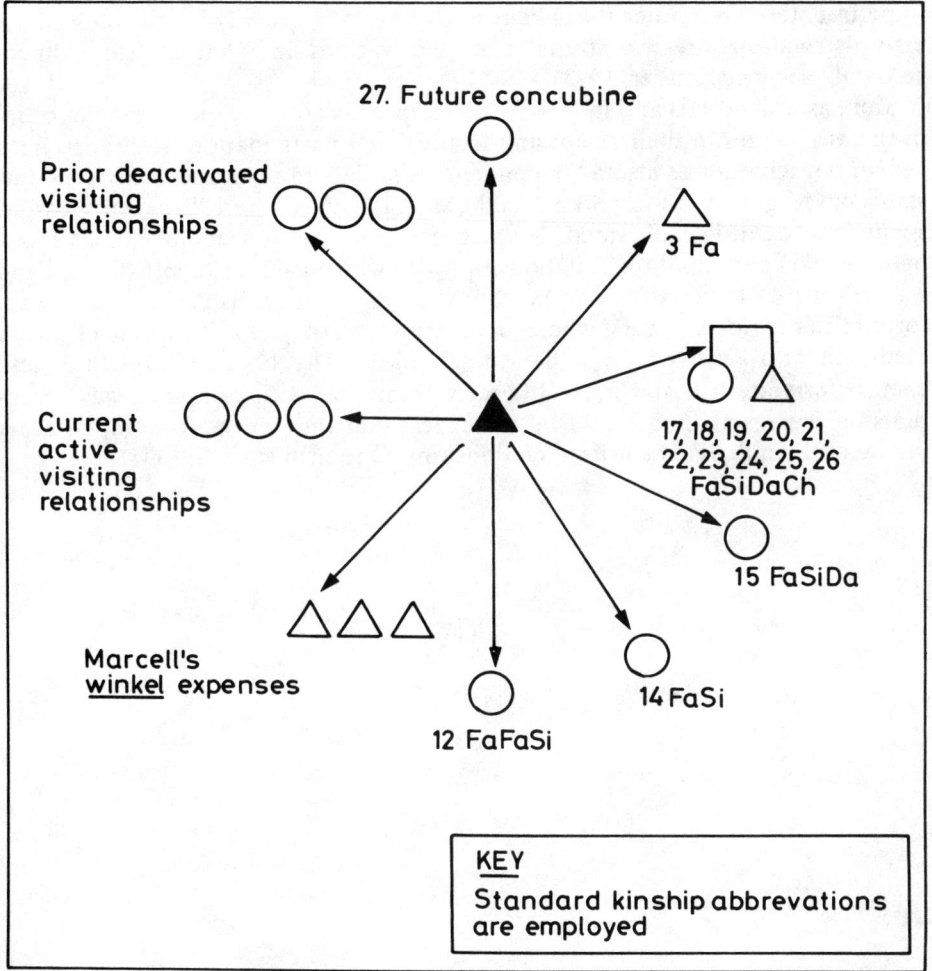

Figure seven Marcell's disbursal patterns

household, according to Buschkens, is therefore a dependent variable responding to disturbances and constraints imposed by the historical and techno-environmental processes of larger society. This, of course, has been known for sometime, though neither Buschkens nor I have gone to any lengths describing macro-structural stresses, strains and deprivations in what is still a "neo-colonial" society (Kruijer, 1973).

Men, as individuals and in groups, develop strategies to cope with erratic and irregular changes in their group and institutional participation. In that respect, *winkel* participation is also a "dependent variable." In response to lay-offs, low status or indignities at the workplace, the shop is a place where "free time" can be spent and identities cultivated. What goes on in the household also affects a man's *winkel* participation. Relationships with women are frequently altered and a man's use of time, space and personnel is temporarily disturbed. The *winkel* forum can provide a context where, in the company of peers, disturbances can be mediated and resolved on a day-to-day basis. The booze, storytelling and camaraderie are fun and make the men "somebodies." A blander way of appraising these activities would be to suggest that they provide "compensatory interaction" in fields of shifting relationships. One such story follows.

Chapter four
Social conflict and ritual restoration: A case of lower-class Creole mating in disequilibrium

> ... beliefs which attribute spiritual power to individuals are never neutral or free of the dominant patterns of social structure. If some beliefs seem to attribute freefloating spiritual powers in a haphazard manner, closer inspection shows consistency. Mary Douglas, *Purity and Danger*.

Men, spinning off from the *winkel* on their various time cycles, establish critical contacts with households. Along these channels flow, reciprocally, vital goods and services. However, these links are tenuous and shifting, denying males a full time (and resource) commitment to any one household and placing them in marginal positions within most of the households where they find themselves at any point in time during their adult life.

Such relationships breed problems; one could call them conflicts of interests. The possible mating arrangements, explored with gusto by men and women, sanction multiple and simultaneous extra-residential and concubinal sexual relationships, which may spawn some hostility and suspicion, and certainly competition, between men and women.[25] For men, whose relationships span many households, the discharge of rights, responsibilities and obligations becomes confusing, conflicting and many times impossible to satisfy. Men are regularly caught between groups of women competing for their resources.

Indeed, many times, the safest place for a male to be is the *winkel*. Although a man can remove himself temporarily, the household process goes on about him. Males must strategically consider their resources: Is it more auspicious to remain with an aunt or to depart with a lover? Are four or five lovers distributed about town better than two located in the neighborhood? How much support should be given to one woman to keep her attached while still leaving enough cash to maintain other women and one's *winkel* life? These problems are usually solved by direct action: the male leaves (or the woman leaves), the male refuses, the male hides, the male disclaims.

Some problems take on a more complex dimension, calling into action supernatural and magical agents. As a number of Afro-Americanists have pointed out, social problems many times result in severe spiritual misfortune and psychological trauma for New World blacks. It is no different for Surinamers (Price, 1976).

This chapter is a description of one man's domestic and household problems. The protagonist, Marcell, resorted to ritual therapy to cope with and solve his dilemma. A magician (*bonoeman*), a marginal and outsider to the neighborhood with no local roots or commitments, was called in to assist Marcell and pull the neighborhood together when it was falling apart. Marcell was engaging in both foolhardy and dangerous behavior and the neighborhood knew it. The *winkel* men and the women made it quite clear in their gossip, admonishments and blunt suggestions that things could not go on as they were. The main problem was Marcell's, stemming directly from his mating patterns; it was also the neighborhood's worry and they, with the ritual expertise of the magician as accelerator, were instrumental in solving it and returning things to "as they should be."

The series of rituals had a definite beginning and end. During this period the social relationships of the major characters, particularly those surrounding the *winkel* and the household, were thrown into sharp relief. The ritual process encapsulated Marcell's life, shed irrelevant mundane matters to reveal the critical supernatural issue and, in short, gave an intense statement of a complex process. Some will read this chapter for "facts" or further information on Surinamese ritual and magical paraphernalia, medicinals, ceremonies, chants or what have you. Camouflaged by the magical goings on, Marcell's story outlines the structural realities — the process — of lower class Creole kinship, domesticity, mating in all its forms, household structure and shifting boundaries, use of time, space and other cultural instrumentalities, neighborhood social organization, and *winkel* life.

Marcell has intimately known a large number of women, some for only moments, one for more than four years. He has provided for all of them and in return for their services has never reneged on his responsibility to contribute to their support. Even after the active phase of a mating relationship has ceased, he was always willing to contribute something if he heard an ex-lover had fallen on hard times.

Seven years before this story, when he was 23 years old, Marcell lived with his paternal aunt Sissy. Sissy's daughter Sadie and her 10 children resided in the house as well and Marcell slept in a small corner of the attic separated by a hanging sheet from the piles of children on the floor. He had a well paying job with a local industry and enjoyed visiting relationships with a number of women.

About this time, Marcell's father moved from his back yard cottage a few blocks away to a new house on the other side of town. Marcell quickly rented the vacated house for Sf 16 per month and used it as his *dorose oso* (outside house), a place where he could bring his girlfriends for privacy. He visited this house two or three times a week, occasionally spending the night. Everyone in the neighborhood knew what he was doing, and would gossip among themselves over Marcell's latest affair.

Marcell maintained his residence at Sissy's. He slept there, ate there, stored all his possessions there, had his laundry and mending done there and contributed heavily to the upkeep of the household and its inhabitants. At this time Sadie did not have a man and the responsibility of maintaining everyone fell in good part on Marcell.

Marcell's *dorose oso* was furnished sparsely. There was nothing in the kitchen save two cups, a plate, a few forks and spoons. A bucket to retrieve water from an outside pump stood on a rickety wooden table. There was no refrigerator or stove and the shelves were empty. The sitting room contained one chair and a mattress. The attic was empty, the floors were uncovered, there were no curtains and the house was filthy. However, it served Marcell just fine.

Marcell has a full brother three years younger than he. This brother was born when Marcell's mother and father were splitting up. Unlike Marcell, he was never legally recognized by the father. The brother bears his mother's name and carries a grudge against Marcell and his father. Marcell and his brother do not speak; Marcell had publicly denounced him as a vagrant. However, they resided in contiguous neighborhoods and, although they did not travel in the same circles, saw each other frequently. When especially pressed the brother often begged money from Marcell.

One Saturday night, a few years ago, Marcell went to the movies and noticed a young Javanese woman.[26] After Creole women, Creole men mate most frequently with Javanese women. They say, "Javanese live like we do and we get along."[27] Marcell made inquiries and found that she lived on the other side of town, came from a very poor family where she resided with her blind mother, two sisters and their men and that she went often to the movies.

Further inquiries informed Marcell that she was a *wakawaka oema* (a walking woman — sexually approachable). Marcell pursued her and, although he never escorted her anywhere, he supplied her with money which she used to buy clothes for herself and food for her family. For more than a year they visited in Marcell's *dorose oso*. They would spend a few hours or the night and when finished would both return to their respective "permanent" residences. At this time Marcell was also visiting other women but felt, because he was supplying her with gifts, that she was not to see any other man.

During his meetings with the woman, he felt moments of intense hostility. Drunk, he would admonish her for her past loose reputation. After treating her deplorably, which occasionally took the form of beatings, he felt guilty, but this emotion quickly evaporated when he learned she was seeing other men behind his back. Her behavior led to further beatings and more guilt. The relationship continued on in this fashion for four years; short visits at the house, hostility and distance, gifts and contributions, and relationships with other men and women, all set in the context of three overlapping households and the larger context of the neighborhood.

Marcell's brother soon entered the picture. Unknown to Marcell he was one of the men sleeping with the Javanese while she was steadily visiting Marcell. The brother often profited from the gifts Marcell gave her. Hostility between Marcell and the brother increased when Marcell discovered that the woman had moved in with the brother while continuing to visit Marcell.

Her situation worsened as the brother, a scoundrel by everyone's definition, denied her support and money in addition to mishandling her. To make ends meet she occasionally approached Marcell at the *winkel* to ask for money. He soon began to blame himself for her plight, feeling he drove her to these terrible circumstances.

After two more years the brother, with no remorse, threw her out. She was temporarily homeless, without income of any sort, uneducated and without skills, sick with tuberculosis and reverting to her old pattern of promiscuity. Marcell felt obliged to do something. It started innocently enough; he wanted to make up for his past behavior and clear his conscience. As he put it, he wanted *lespeki foe en srefi* (self-respect).

Marcell formulated a plan and suggested it to the men at the *winkel*. He devised a rehabilitation program and arranged for the woman to get a morning job as a maid and go to school in the afternoon to learn Dutch and mathematics. He would pay her tuition and buy her books. He made arrangements to have her tuberculosis treated. Then, after she had completed school, he would send her to Holland to work. This would involve buying her clothes and luggage, arranging transportation and finding her housing and work. Friends recently returned from Holland suggested that she might work as a nurse's aide. Marcell agreed and estimated he would need about Sf 1600 ($820) in about six months' time to put his scheme into operation.

The *winkel* men scoffed at the idea. Why should Marcell feel committed to her, especially when he would get no return on his investment? The question of his responsibility was glossed over and everyone agreed Marcell would be foolishly wasting money. Why, he didn't even have any children with her. The crew tried to dissuade him but soon gave up. In his absence the men would shake their heads lamenting Marcell's crazy plans. Word spread throughout the neighborhood.

Marcell intensified his visiting relationships with the woman and promised her there would be no more beatings and that he would indulge her. She in turn promised to go faithfully to work and school, visit the doctor regularly and not *waka waka* anymore. She did not address the question of going to Holland.

A week or two later he found out from one of the *winkel* men that the woman was seen downtown during her work hours. Checking with her employer he found out she had quit. Further investigations proved she was not attending school regularly and that she did not show up for tuberculosis treatments. The *winkel* men threw this in Marcell's face. "You see," they said, "She is only using you and your money. Women aren't worth it." "No," replied Marcell, "she is only dumb and ignorant and must be trained." In Marcell's estimation she was not responsible for her behavior.

An incident, started by the brother, aggravated the issue. The atmosphere of the *winkel* was charged with Marcell's story. One evening while a sizable portion of the group was assembled the brother entered. Sneering and offensive he accused Marcell of stupidity and naivete. If he wanted to give his money to a worthless whore and be exploited by her that was his business. Furthermore, who did he think he was determining people's destinies with his opinions and charity. The *winkel* regulars remained silent while outsiders added their commentary to the brother's.

When the brother called him a dumb Negro trying to play God, Marcell sprang from his seat. Grabbing a heavy glass top from an apothocary jar on the counter he lunged at his brother and tried to smash his head in. Fortunately, a friend was standing between them and caught Marcell in midair. Pinning his arms back and shouting at the brother to leave, he was joined by the other *winkel* men. Both shamed and infuriated, Marcell left accompanied by the yells of the *winkel* men telling him not to seek out his brother.

Spending more time together, but not yet living in concubinage, Marcell began contributing more to the woman's upkeep. Aside from giving her Sf 50 every fortnight, a sizable sum, he would often be called upon to pay new tuition installments and buy books. With every paycheck he set aside money for her ticket to Holland. Everyone in the neighborhood was watching and men and women alike agreed Marcell was being exploited.

Early one October afternoon, four months after the incident with his brother, Marcell stalked sullenly into the *winkel* clutching a knife.

He was quickly surrounded by his friends Schill, Chris and Rijker. Hearing his story they agreed he was about to do something very foolish. Earlier in the day he had gone to his woman's sister's house to try and locate his lover. A neighbor told him that the woman no longer lived there, but further down the street in the house of another man. Marcell went to the location and found the house empty. Looking about, he discovered her clothing, male articles and bills for large expenditures. The contributions he had made to her were going in part to support another man.

A man entered and Marcell asked if he was living with the Javanese. Recognizing Marcell the man began pleading with Marcell not to beat him. He admitted living with her and buying things for himself with Marcell's money. Marcell's wrath, however, was not for him.

Running home to his house he grabbed a small kitchen knife and ran up the street to the *winkel* yelling for everyone to hear that he was going to "cut off her arm." Although ostensibly looking for the woman he went directly to the *winkel* and was easily lured inside by the *winkel* men. There they tried to calm him. One cannot trust a woman anyway so what did he expect? There are plenty of women in Paramaribo. Marcell would be much better off if he would just go out and look for another that would appreciate him. "Don't worry," interjected a friend, "maybe the woman abused you but you can get her back by running around with every female you meet." Finally Schill reached down, took the knife from Marcell and gave it to Chris for safe keeping.

A lot of people knew of Marcell's plight. Although it angered him that his name was bantered about, he used these networks to spread news of his intentions and, in this case, to force people to intercede and stop him from doing something that would have had extra-neighborhood consequences (e.g., the police and state legal machinery). The neighborhood was alive with stories. Everyone thought that Marcell should drop the woman immediately. Marcell was adamant. Cooling off, he decided that the woman did not know what she was doing and it was his obligation to care for her. She must be sent to Holland immediately, whether she had a job, the requisite skills or not. The men rose in a clamor. Marcell was beyond help.

He took the next morning off from work, gathered her birth registry book and papers and went to get her a passport. At the government office everything went smoothly until he was questioned about her health. He lied about any contagious illnesses but a suspicious government official checked with the Health Office and found that she was still undergoing treatment. Marcell was denied the passport.

Marcell decided that he must keep the woman in his care. This time he exacted a promise that she would live with her sister, stop visiting the man with whom she had been living and visit no other men except Marcell. This most recent male interloper was not heard from again.

From the knife incident in October until mid-December, Marcell frequently and regularly visited the Javanese woman in the *dorose oso*. He continued to make his contributions. All proceeded without mishap.

Early in December the woman told Marcell that her sister had been evicted and forced to move into a smaller house. There was no room for her to stay on with her sister. She begged Marcell if she could stay, just for a short time, in his *dorose oso* house. Realizing the implications of this move, Marcell agreed. Shortly thereafter she moved in all her possessions and set up residence. Marcell continued to live at his aunt's house.

During that month the house took on more and more of a woman's touch. In fact she became a model homemaker, much unlike her former self. She was settling in. Curtains appeared and a gas bomb was bought. The mattress was brought up to the attic and placed on a bed frame and kitchen utensils appeared in the cooking area. For Marcell, these items would keep her at home and away from the "bad influences" of Paramaribo. There was talk of Holland, but the plans became more diffuse. She did not want to go.

In early January Sissy's granddaughter Mabel fell ill. It was uncertain whether it was a *datra siekie* (physical illness responsive to a western physician's care) or a *nengre siekie* (a spiritual illness caused by supernatural agents). She needed care (and was treated by both doctors and local curers) and was brought downstairs and placed on the large double bed in the sitting room. Four children were forced to sleep in the attic. There was no room left for Marcell in the small house. He moved out and in with the Javanese woman.

From January to July he lived out his normal routine in the neighborhood. Only his place of residence had changed. He still contributed regularly (though not as much) to Sissy's house and took occasional meals there. Over the course of the next few months he gradually moved more of his possessions to his house. His *winkel* attendance fell off slightly as he began to spend more intimate time with his lover; however, he still was a full-time *winkel* participant.

One July evening Marcell, before leaving to go out for a drink, gave the woman Sf 5 for her to go to the movies alone. He told her to be home early and not to talk to anyone.

The next morning found him at the *winkel*. Instead of going to work, he was sitting there livid with rage. When he had come home at 1 o'clock the night before he found the house open with no one there. Arising late the next morning he found the woman still not back. He asked neighbors if she had gone out early and they all replied that they had not seen her. Intuition and experience suggested he look for her at her sister's house.

Entering the sister's yard he heard a warning shout of his presence. Before he was able to phrase a question the sister ran toward him, blocked the doorway and told him his woman was not there. Pushing her aside he marched into the three-room cottage and saw a man in his underwear lying on the bed with his back turned. His woman was huddled in the corner wearing only a man's undershirt. Thinking the Creole man on the mat was the sister's man he paid no attention and merely was irritated with the woman for not coming home.

A closer look at the man exposed him as Marcell's brother. Realizing what had happened he threatened the brother with a beating if he ever interfered in his affairs again. Turning to the woman he ordered her to retrieve her clothes from his house and never to return again. Storming out of the house he cursed the sister for condoning such behavior.

Outside in the yard Creole and Javanese neighbors gathered. They applauded Marcell for his actions and called out that the woman had been shamed mightily. This story would spread quickly.

Marcell returned to the *winkel* and told the story to the crew members present. The men shook their heads in disbelief; how could one brother treat another in such a disgraceful manner? Something was amiss; things like this are not supposed to happen. It was hard for them to believe, but it was only an extreme version of an often cited proverb: When you do good you get bad in return (*Te joe doe boen joe e kisi ogri baka*).[28] After Marcell's departure the men could hardly hide their nervous laughter. Marcell was a sucker, both for the woman and the brother.

From his work in the interior Marcell had developed an acquaintance with a Bush Negro from the Saramaka tribe.[29] Moving to the city, this man had capitalized on his tribal stereotype in Creole eyes as a man familiar with the deep ways of the supernatural and had become a *bonoeman* (magician).[30]

For two days Marcell mulled over his plight. He felt the causes were not as clear cut as originally perceived. He decided to seek the advice of the *bonoeman*. He was beginning to speak more of revenge; he felt abused and was in a confused state of mind.

Marcell told the *bonoeman* his tale from beginning to end. Shaking his head the *bonoeman* concurred that there was more to the problem than met the eye. Spiritual and supernatural forces were at work and Marcell had to respond in kind. Through the *bonoeman's* suggestions Marcell decided that magical spells were being cast upon him and the woman. He suspected that she was no longer in control of her senses but was being manipulated by the brother. Marcell devised the following strategy to which the *bonoeman* agreed.[31]

The first matter at hand was to break the spell cast on the woman. Marcell was to take all her clothing except for two pieces of underwear and place them outside the door of his house. The undergarments were to be placed under the sitting room linoleum, and everyone who is a friend of Marcell's must walk on them. This was to accomplish three things: break her spirit (*broko en geest, meki en saka*), force her to fail at whatever attempts she makes contrary to Marcell's wishes and assure Marcell complete power over her for his ends.

Marcell also had to take precautions to protect himself. A future date was set when he would be given a charm (*tapoe*) and a ritual washing (*wasi skin*) to protect him from any *wisi* (sorcery) his brother might work against him.

Wishing to hurt his brother in some manner, Marcell wanted the power to have sexual access to and control over any female his brother engaged in the future. In addition, Marcell wanted sexual access to the woman's sister. This is a form of revenge as well as control since she lied to Marcell and sanctioned his woman's extra-residential affair in her home.

The wheels were in motion and the problem shifted from the secular to the supernatural. There were unseen connections between events that Marcell and the *bonoeman* had to identify. That night Marcell placed the undergarments under his linoleum and walked upon them. From that point on, all behavior was interpreted in terms of the supernatural and its forces. Events were not as they seemed, or as they had once been explained. Everything done to Marcell or by Marcell would be interpreted on a different order of reality. In many ways, everything done and to be done would become a self-fulfilling prophecy.

Two days after he placed the underwear under the linoleum the woman returned. While she was in the house Marcell took her upstairs and had intercourse with her. Her return and the sex act proved to Marcell that he had regained control over her. Every morning thereafter she would return to spend half the day cleaning and cooking whether Marcell was home or not.

Not trusting her he followed her to school later that week and found his brother waiting for her. Obviously his brother was working some particularly evil spell on the girl, much stronger than the ceremony Marcell had performed to get her back. He understood he had failed to break his brother's hold. Yet, it was even more evident that he was wrong in chastising the woman; she was obviously not responsible for her behavior in light of the brother's power. Marcell demanded control over the woman stronger than that of the brother's. The *bonoeman* would have to provide more powerful magic. Marcell decided to consult the *bonoeman* the next day.

Early the next morning he stopped at the *winkel* for a drink. There he found his father, who was in one of his rare states of good health, waiting for him. The old man knew of Marcell's problem and came to talk with him. They discussed the problem in detail and the father agreed that Marcell's course of action was justifiable.

He left for the *bonoeman's* house, a small, run-down barrack located behind a weathered street-front house. It was almost barren of furnishings. Two hammocks were strung from the walls, while benches, empty bottles, glasses and plates lay in disarray on the floor. A kerosene lantern illuminated the darked room.

Two women, barebreasted and wrapped in cloth around their waists, sat combing their hair with wooden combs. The *bonoeman*, on hearing Marcell's story, pointed out that the first ritual to bring the woman back had temporarily worked, although it was not strong enough to keep her permanently out of the clutches of the brother. The most important matter, suggested the *bonoeman,* was to protect Marcell from *wisi* worked by his brother. The ceremonial washing, however, could not be done today because the *bonoeman's jeje* (spirit — one of the functionally specific compartments of the soul) was not settled and comfortable. Should he perform the washing today, it would not work.

This turned out to be a pattern. Whenever Marcell asked the *bonoeman* to perform a certain ritual to assure a certain event, the *bonoeman* consistently made an excuse to temporarily delay the ceremony. Doubtless this was to give him time to investigate the case and, after hearing the gossip and learning the circumstances, decide on the feasibility of the request and the odds of the goal actually materializing. If he thought the chances were good that it would "work out" he would perform the ceremony; otherwise he would try to dissuade Marcell.

The *bonoeman* suggested that they set the washing ceremony for Friday night. This would given him time to spiritually recuperate and also to purchase the items necessary for the rite. Before leaving the *bonoeman* delivered a lengthy speech on his own character. He emphasized that he was honest, reliable and not greedy. He never sought to rob people or take advantage of their weakened condition. (People in Suriname are often victimized by crooked *bonoemen*, who extort great amounts of money. Magic can be quite a "racket," and Creoles are rightfully suspicious of approaching a *bonoeman* they do not know.) The *bonoeman* said that he would charge nothing for the ritual washing but "would take what Marcell's soul wanted to give him" (*Mie sa teki san joe jeje e gi mie*). Marcell found this agreeable. He left relieved by the conviction that by the weekend everything would be back in order.

All the next week, before the rite, the Javanese woman came to his house. Although he would not permit her to stay he was slowly changing his mind. She was a good woman, he thought, and if he could only be assured that he had full control over her she would be nice to have around.

The ritual to bring the woman back was working. Supposedly she knew nothing about it. However, she was privy to neighborhood gossip and stories had been spreading that Marcell was up to something. Also, knowing Marcell she expected him to dabble with the supernatural. Marcell's behavior was strange. Upon her return in the mornings he would cockily announce, "I knew you would return; it had to be." Following ritual dictum she was always rewarded with a few guilders.

Friday afternoon Marcell went to the *bonoeman's* to arrange a time and place for the ceremony. Explaining the week's events, the *bonoeman* was pleased to hear how the woman was returning regularly, thus confirming Marcell's partial control over her.

A list was drawn up and Marcell was told to buy the following items tomorrow at the central market: spoon (*nang spoon*), 1 plate (*nang preti*), 1 piece of sugar cane (*pisi chen*), 1 parrot tail feather (*popokai teri*), and 1 Indian clay pot (*prapi*). The *bonoeman* would bring peanuts, sugar, ritual grasses (*wiwiri*) and other items.

Much relieved, Marcell retired to the *winkel* to tell his story to the assembled men. Very little was said in his presence other than that he should be very careful. When Marcell was not at the *winkel* his story was debated endlessly and with fervor as everyone evaluated the situation from the past, present and future perspectives. Marcell was dealing with supernatural agents and one mishap or error could bring misfortune to him and perhaps others. The supernatural world is capricious, unpredictable and not entirely understood by mortals. Marcell's life was laid open in the public forum. Word even reached Sissy and Sadie some blocks away. They complained that he was foolish spending all his money on the woman and it would be better if he gave it to them.

The *bonoeman* arrived at the house 8 o'clock Sunday night. The Javanese, who was there cleaning, saw him enter the yard carrying all of his paraphenalia. Marcell was cold and aloof with her and, as the *bonoeman* entered the house, he gave her money to go to the movies. The woman was quite shaken; she knew a *bonoeman* when she saw one. As the woman went out the door the *bonoeman* sat down and began assembling his items. To Marcell's acquisitions he added a handful of powdered rice, three pieces of raw cassava, a ten cent piece (*dubbeltje*), a pile of sugar, a handful of shucked peanuts and a braided circular mat the size of a saucer.

The *bonoeman* instructed Marcell to make a watery mix in the pot composed of all the items except the parrot tail feather. After washing with the concoction each morning, he must dip the tail feather in the mixture, place it in his mouth and either ask for good things to come his way (*boen sani gi joe screfi*) or curse others (*cos-cosi tra soema*).This must be done everyday for a month.

The *bonoeman* then asked if the brother was really Marcell's brother. Marcell told him it was true and that they both came from the same mother and father. Hearing this the *bonoeman* jumped from his chair and declared this impossible; brothers could not treat themselves in such a manner. He said, "There is no better thing than your own brother" (*No wan moro boen sani de leki brada*). (In Suriname half brothers, especially those from different mothers, are not close and many times do not even know each other. Many Creoles feel that since they are related through the father you really cannot be sure if they are in fact brothers.)

The *bonoeman* looked Marcell in the eye and said he had a few suggestions for him. Did he not think, surmised the *bonoeman,* that it would be better if he took the woman back to live with him again. He was providing her with money and goods and it would be safer, as she is a weak person and possibly still under the partial control of the brother, if he brought her in and kept an eye on her (*hori en boen*). He could then be sure she would go to her lessons, not consort with other men and make preparations to send her to Holland. Marcell acquiesced and, when the women came by the next day, he told her she could sleep there with him.

Monday, Tuesday and Wednesday passed without incident. The woman busied herself around the house and shopped; the only thing that distinguished her from being an ideal concubine was that she went to school. She was given strict instructions not to touch the *prapi* and its contents.

Thursday it happened again. It would soon be clear to everyone that even stronger measures would have to be taken in what was turning out to be a very complicated circumstance. That night at 5 p.m. Marcell returned from work and, before going to the *winkel,* told the woman to have food waiting for him upon his return about 10 p.m. She agreed but said she would have to go to class that night. Could Marcell give her Sf 25 for fees due? He gave her the money and left. Returning late that night he found that the woman still had not returned. He rushed up the street to the woman's mother's cottage and looking in through the broken shutters, saw the woman and his brother lying in bed together. Screaming and smashing the window he called for the brother to come out of the house and fight. In the ensuing hub-bub the woman dashed out the window screaming for the police.

Marcell knew better than to enter the mother's house uninvited as that was a criminal offense. Bellowing that he would kill the brother he was interrupted by the police. Reports from the neighbors and the looks on the antagonists' faces told the police this was no light matter. All three were brought to the police station to file a report.

Sitting before two Creole detectives the brother began charging Marcell with assault with intent to kill. Marcell remained calm and in control. The police asked to whom the woman belonged and Marcell claimed her as he provides for her. The police asked who she was sleeping with and Marcell tipped his head towards his brother. Shocked and disgusted the detectives sent the brother out of the room. They had handled cases like this many times before, but never with blood brothers. They proceeded to interrogate the woman in the Dutch language. In her nervous state she was unable to respond with coherency in what for her was a foreign language. They asked the following questions:

"Were you sleeping with the brother last night?"
"Yes."
"Had you been living with Marcell?"
"Yes."
"Did he give you money for lessons?"
"Yes."
"Did he give you spending money?"
"Yes."
"Did he buy you food and clothes?"
"Yes."
"Does the brother give you anything?"
"No."
„Do you want to live with Marcell again?"
"No."
"Do you want to lock Marcell up?"
"Yes."

The police were bewildered with this series of answers and obviously disgusted with her behavior. They accused her of being crazy (as everyone had been doing lately) for leaving a man who provided for her and going off to live with a bum. They told her that if they heard of her again they would lock her up in the local mental asylum. With that they sent her away. The police made obvious where their sentiments lay. They acknowledged to Marcell that his brother was using the woman to siphon off his moneys. They condemned her mightily for male reasons.

They asked Marcell if he still wanted her and he replied with an emphatic no. He was to control himself, said the police, for if he hurt her they would have to arrest him. He was told to bundle up her possessions and send for someone to retrieve them. Two officers would stop by later the next day to make sure everything went off as planned. As he left, they wished him well, sympathizing with his plight. Women, they agreed, were crazy.

Marcell decided that this latest scandal was the last straw. With morning light he made a stop at the travel agency to pick up his ticket deposit for the woman's emigration to Holland. Arriving at the *winkel* he sent a small boy to tell the *bonoeman* there were new developments and they must talk. Taking a drink, before returning home to await the police, he told the men at the *winkel* that he had had enough and that his only desired revenge now was to make the woman his complete slave.

Marcell bought a bottle of rum and returned to his house. While bundling up her clothes the two officers arrived. In a very official manner they seated themselves, withdrew paper and pencil and began a very formal interrogation. Marcell told them nothing about the magic.

While Marcell was reciting the sequence of events, the Creole officer began nervously twitching about in his seat and sniffing the air. Craning his head over the back of the seat he looked directly into the fermenting *prapi*. Evidently the officer thought he was in a situation where the formal judicial canons of Dutch law would be of little use. He closed his notebook, stopped Marcell's tale and told the other officer they must quickly leave. They left abruptly. (Police have often been the victims of sorcery.)

Losing patience waiting for someone to retrieve the woman's clothes, Marcell picked up the bundle stuffed with clothing and dashed out the door. Sauntering up the middle of the street to the woman's mother's house he yelled obscenities and informed all interested parties (of which there were many as the street was lined with heads popped out of windows) of his latest mishap. Marcell strewed the woman's clothing in the street and the gutter. A trail of garments left a path from Marcell's house to the mother's. Although the street was full of people the garments were not touched.

Marcell retired to the *winkel*. Half an hour later a police car containing two different officers, the woman and the brother pulled up. Curtly they ordered Marcell into the car and to the police station. His brother and woman called the police to arrest Marcell for willful destruction of property. Marcell had to be hauled bodily into the car by the two officers. The men looked on. None tried nor were expected to help.

Marcell was brought to the station held by one of the officers. Once out of the car he loosed himself from the grip and flew into a rage, kicking, biting and punching everyone within striking distance. Policemen charged from the building and, some with billy clubs beat him into submission. None of the officers knew of Marcell's plight and they treated him as a common troublemaker.

Once upstairs Marcell was brought before the two Creole detectives who originally handled his case. They apologized profusely for his treatment at the hands of the police and tried to calm him. There was nothing the police could do except, once again, castigate the brother and woman. Cautioning Marcell not to physically harm them, the detectives devised a plan that would soothe Marcell's thirst for revenge. If the woman or the brother ever came to Marcell's house again, he was to immediately call the police and they would see to it that the couple was sent to the local insane asylum. As for the officers that beat Marcell, the detectives could do nothing.

Marcell was confused and belligerent. He refused a ride home. Before collapsing in exhaustion at home he sent one last message to the *bonoeman*. It was imperative that they meet the next morning. Missing work did not deter Marcell in pursuing his grand design.

Saturday morning Marcell waited at home for the *bonoeman*.

He had decided on a course of action and would propose it for advice and counsel. He wanted to exact revenge on the police who beat him up and also assure that this sort of thing would never happen again. He also wanted to bring the woman back to his house one more time. This accomplished he would make her his slave and drive her crazy. It is interesting to note that when Marcell explained what he would do to her when he made her his slave, the behavior differed very little from her regular housewoman role.

Getting impatient, Marcell decided to walk to the *bonoeman's* house. Once there, he brought the *bonoeman* up to date on the new developments; the woman had once again fallen into the clutches of the brother and the incident at the police station. Marcell implied that the *bonoeman* was not as powerful as he had first thought.

With an air of authority motivated in part by indignation the *bonoeman* gave forth with a disclaimer. Did not Marcell realize that the ritual performed had worked, for in fact the woman had returned. Just because she left again was no reason for alarm. No ritual, he pointed out, is permanent; it may work for one day, one week, or one month and anybody that tells you differently is a liar. Marcell was put at ease.

The *bonoeman* was confident. The rituals would be performed that very night. For the ceremony against the police Marcell must find a flat stone, a rooster tail feather and a ripe calabash gourd. In addition, Marcell must write the woman's name on a sheet of paper along with a summons ordering her return.

Nervous that something might go wrong, Marcell said he wanted to write the message then and there and have the *bonoeman* approve it. Pen and paper in hand Marcell wrote the following:

5 Augustus	5 August
Kiram Sadodiroro	Kiram Sadodiroro
Mie abi joe fanodoe.	I have need of you.
Joe moesoe kon na mie	You must come to my
oso esi-esi	house quickly.
van Dyke, Marcell	van Dyke, Marcell

"Yes," said the bonoeman, "that would surely work."

It is important to note that this is the first time Marcell or the *bonoeman* (or any other Creoles aside from the police) ever used the woman's legal name. For this brief ritual she became a "person." At the completion of the ritual she became, once again, "the woman."

The *bonoeman* arrived promptly at 7 p.m. and began with instructions immediately. At night, when everyone in the neighborhood is asleep, Marcell must dig a round hole one foot in diameter before his doorstep. He must then sprinkle half of a bottle of raw rum about the hole and invoke the spirit of the Ground Mother (*Gron Mama*) by chanting, "You have lived here for so long I need you" (*Joe ben libi djaso someni langa, mi abi joe fanodoe*). Then he must take a bread roll (*puntbrood*), cut it in two pieces, eat half and place the other half in the hole. He then must place the note he wrote earlier in the day on top of the bread, sprinkle the remainder of the rum on the articles and while filling the hole recite the following:

Mi nanga a meisje ben	This woman and I have
njan djaso someni langa	eaten her for so long.

meki en jeje kon njan djaso baka. Joe ben libi djaso fosi ten, noe joe moesoe kon libi nanga mi baka. Kon njan a brede mie ben seti gi joe.	Force her "soul" to come eat here again. You have lived here earlier, now you must come live with me again. Come and eat the bread I have set for you.

To be double safe Marcell was told to do something that would keep the woman away from the bother. Tomorrow he must buy lemon juice and gunpowder (*kroiti*). He must mix them together in a potion and paint the mixture in a circle around the brother's house. The woman will be unable to cross over the line. Marcell did that the following night.

The ritual to protect Marcell from ever again suffering at the hands of the police followed. The *bonoeman* was confident; he had performed this ritual many times and it always worked. In fact, the day before he had performed a similar ceremony for a well-to-do mulatto lady who sought a favorable decision in a court case. The ritual, quite broad in scope, may be tailored to fit the situation.

Placing the stone in the middle of the table, he emptied a pile of dried seed kernels called *nengre kondre pepre* from the vial onto the stone. Taking up a handful of grass (*man grasi*) the *bonoeman* began twisting and brading it into long strangs. Chanting in Saramakan, his tribal language, he tied the stone with the grass strands, untied it, and ordered the powers to make Marcell's spirit stay outside the stone. Tying the knot fast he ordered that the trouble between Marcell and the police stay inside the stone.

He then handed Marcell four *nengre kondre pepre* and told him to chew and spit the remains on the stone while he and *bonoeman* continued to chant. Tomorrow morning when it is still dark, Marcell must take the stone and four more kernals of the *pepre* to the river and there repeat the spitting. Before he throws the stone in the water say, "What you want to make the police incident abate" (*San joe wani foe kowroe a skotoe tori*). (A number of ceremonies use the river to carry away unwanted problems, annoying spirits and malevolent ancestral ghosts.) Marcell followed the instructions the next morning.

Marcell was pleased and confidently told the *bonoeman* he knew the woman would return so that he would kill her. With this the *bonoeman* jumped from his seat and told Marcell that he must not do this for it is "bad" (*ogri*) and that he did not want his *wisi* used to kill people. Perhaps, the *bonoeman* suggested, Marcell should stay with his original plan and only try to drive her mad. Marcell agreed.

Marcell retired to the *winkel* and found only teenagers playing cards. They made a few inquiries and Marcell brought them up to date, to their surprised exclamations. The *wisi* story would spread; trouble was brewing. At this point also Marcell was averaging about three days a week at work. He told his foreman, a Creole, that he had a "need" (*fanodoe*) and the man understood entirely.

Sunday afternoon found Marcell in the *winkel*. He mentioned the rituals performed the night before and that earlier today he had failed to find the *bonoeman*. He was sitting with Schill, Elder, Frankie and Chris and the conversation at hand jumped from topic to topic avoiding Marcell's affairs. By 9 o'clock in the evening the crowd left. Marcell had been uncommonly distant, disagreeable and quiet all day.

As it turned out, last night after the ceremony Marcell had a dream. (Dreams are relied on heavily for their suggestive and informative powers.) In the dream, the brother, the woman and Marcell's half sister (she had a reputation of dabbling in the black arts) passed before Marcell each carrying a bouquet of jasmine, *fayalobi* and *dede roetoe* (death root). They said nothing in the dream, a clear symbol of imminent death.

The dream once again changed Marcell's evaluation of the woman's behavior: She was not responsible for her behavior but, rather, under the heavy spell of the *wisi*-working brother. Again she was forgiven. Although he was angry and hurt, he convinced himself she was only innocently acting out the commands of others. To rectify the situation he decided he could stop at nothing short of capturing her soul.

Monday evening he told his story in the *winkel* and pointed out for everyone to hear that he was no longer so angry with the woman. She was weak and dumb and it was the brother who was entirely at fault. She, he surmised, had to be cared for. That evening Marcell went to the *bonoeman* and told him of the dream and his interpretation. The *bonoeman* agreed to the ceremony to capture the girl's soul. Tomorrow night at 8 o'clock they would meet. Word of this arrangement was already being passed through the neighborhood by everyone who had been in the *winkel*.

The next day Marcell arrived at the *winkel* at 5 o'clock and drank there heavily for three hours. Home, he found the *bonoeman* pacing impatiently in his yard. They entered the house and got down to business in the privacy of the upstairs sleeping room.

The *bonoeman* identified the items he had brought along. One *pimba* block and *pimba* powder (ceremonial white powder, the consistency of chalk, used in many Creole rituals), one porcelain Chinese rice bowl (*komki*), one *papa moni* shell, one ten cent piece, one egg, one parrot tail feather (*popokai teri*), one handkerchief, three vials of perfume, one bundle of grass (*san' grafoe wiwiri*), three drinking tumblers and a bucket filled with water from the pump in Marcell's yard. Marcell nervously sat on the edge of the bed and watched the *bonoeman* intently.

Turning to Marcell, the *bonoeman* asked him on what day the woman was born. Marcell told him Saturday and the *bonoeman* replied that throughout the following ceremony the woman would be referred to by her Afro-Creole day name "Kwamina."

This is the second and last time the woman was referred to by a name. It is important to note that she was given an Afro-Creole ritual name and, at least, symbolically drawn into the Creole group and made subject to Creole rules and regulations. When *bonoemen* provide services (spirit dances, post-mortem rites, therapeutic or evil magic) for their clients, they usually do not use the person's Christian name, but employ the spiritually powerful day name. At least one opposition, Creole-Javanese, was dropped from consideration in this case.

Beginning to chant in Saramakan, the *bonoeman* called out "Kwamina" and told her to return to take her money. Repeating this over and over in a low-excited voice he set about creating a symbolic relief, constructed of the materials he brought, on the floor. Abruptly ceasing his chant he ordered Marcell to take a chair, place it over the symbol and sit. Marcell began perspiring profusely as his breathing quickened and his eyes narrowed. The *bonoeman* then broke a vial of perfume and dumped its musky contents on Marcell's bare chest. Marcell gasped and jumped. As the room became filled with the cheap suffocating vapors, the *bonoeman* began commanding the spirit of the woman to return. Ordering Marcell to extent his arm full length, the *bonoeman* balanced a bowl filled with water in which an egg was placed in Marcell's upturned palm. The slightest quiver would spill the water over the brim. The muscles of Marcell's forearms, biceps and shoulders tightened as he stared intensely at the still container. Not a drop spilled.

After 15 minutes of chanting and incantation, admonishing, cajoling and enjoining the woman, Marcell's arm was still steady. The *bonoeman* continued for 10 more minutes now suggesting that the water was spilling. Marcell had been holding his arm in such a fashion for almost half an hour.

The bowl quivered slightly and one droplet ran over the side. Seeing this the *bonoeman* began yelling. "She is here, she is here." Marcell started, spilled the liquid, and let out a blood-curdling scream. Rising from his chair he smashed the bowl against the wall and fell flailing to the floor. Marcell then passed out for twenty minutes, indicating that he had drawn the woman into himself. The *bonoeman* revived Marcell by rubbing the juices from some crushed grasses between his toes and on his eyelids. It was clear from Marcell's violent reaction that the brother had been working some magic against him, but all was right now, as the *bonoeman* had removed the woman's spirit from the brother's hands and placed it in Marcell's charge.

If properly executed a magical ceremony secures the desired ends. Barring contingencies such as competition from another magician, the ritual participant merely follows the rules, both supernatural and secular, set down by the magician and his wishes must materialize.

The day after the ritual was performed Marcell blundered. He did not give the "supernatural agents" time to work but, in a fit of anger and frustration, took matters into his own hands and upset the processes at work.

That evening Marcell was walking to the *winkel* and passed a restaurant that he had passed everyday for the last six years. Casually looking inside he was shocked to see the Javanese woman working inside selling sundries; the last job he remembered her having. Rushing to the bar he demanded to know what she was doing. Word got to the *winkel* and triggered the evening's discussion. Everyone knew she was supposed to come to Marcell and not he to her.

Marcell spent the evening deep in conversation with the woman. She was hostile and would not meet his eyes when he addressed her. He was ashamed that his ex-woman (and the one he wanted back) would be working at such a menial job in a public place. He had given her the opportunity to better herself, go to school, live in a comfortable well-provisioned home and eventually go to Holland. She gave no explanation, telling him only to go away.

Hearing this, Marcell turned and in wide-eyed amazement said, "She is crazy, I know my brother made her crazy." For the next hour he insisted on telling her, and anyone else who would listen, that she was crazy. He promised that if she came back to him he would make her better and see to it she was cured.

Marcell was convinced of foul play. "You see," he pointed out, "it is not her I am talking to, but to something evil." He gave up and went outside to smoke a cigarette. Shortly after he called her outside and, taking two one hundred guilder notes from his pocket thrust them in her hand, and told her to take care of herself. She refused saying she didn't want Marcell or his money. What magic, thought Marcell, would make a woman give back Sf 200? After much banter she finally accepted the proffered cash.

Marcell justified the transaction by saying that in her state she would doubtless give the money to the brother who would spend it on food, drink and clothing for himself. This would give Marcell an edge in gaining control over him.

Marcell asked to be taken to the *bonoeman* immediately. Before the *bonoeman* he poured forth his story. The *bonoeman,* with a look of dismay on his face, calmed him and said he would go with Marcell that very minute and perform a ritual to resolve this problem.

Sitting in front of the shop the *bonoeman* said that this was going to be a very difficult case as Marcell had caused enough trouble already (*toemsi foeroe trobi kaba*). It is better, said the *bonoeman,* if he would behave more discretely and mind his manners and have respect for people. Marcell's behavior was going against the grain of magic. The *bonoeman* gave an example of a case he had just completed. If a woman leaves, you should go about getting her back softly and slowly, following the advice of a man "who knows things."

The *bonoeman* decided Marcell was about to ruin everything and entered the bar. Interrupting Marcell's barrage of insults, he smiled kindly at the woman and asked how she was. Recognizing the *bonoeman* she dropped her eyes and politely responded. He asked her what was wrong and she said that she did not want to live with Marcell. Raising his eyebrows in mock surprise, and now almost saccharine in his kindness, the *bonoeman* smiled, touched her lightly on the shoulder and said, "But you will, you will."

At the house, the *bonoeman* laid out the ingredients for the ceremony to once again recapture the woman. There was one rooster tail feather, a bottle of lavender lotion, *nengre kondre pepre* and a black substance that had the consistency of wet steel wool. Marcell retrieved the calabash he had cut the week before and a pair of the woman's soiled underwear he had hidden. A powerful ceremony was undertaken to assure that the woman would return. An hour later the ritual drew to a close and Marcell, much relieved, gave the *bonoeman* an unsolicited Sf 25. Before leaving the *bonoeman* reminded him that under no circumstances was he to visit the woman again or attempt to contact her in any way. She would return.

Marcell followed the man's orders to the letter. His free time was spent at the *winkel* men knew the woman, whom the brother had just impregnated, Marcell woman away from his brother and discussed the story with the men. A number of *winkel* men knew the woman, whom the brother had just impregnated, Marcell had in mind. She would soon hear of Marcell's plans.

Saturday morning Marcell was awakened by noises downstairs. It was the Javanese woman. She claimed she had returned only to give him some vegetables she had bought. She explained she had spent Sf 50 of the money he had given her on school fees and medical costs, but would give the rest back. Marcell was no longer under the spell of his brother. They continued to talk and Marcell was astonished by her pleasant conduct and manners. She was herself; even better.

Sunday, the day after the last ceremony, Marcell threw out the *prapi* used in the washing ceremony. He felt he no longer needed a protective charm. However, he refused to remove the calabash used in her latest "return" ceremony. He had been mistaken before. Although she protested and said the calabash frightened her (*Mie skin e gro te mie sie en*), Marcell was adamant.

Monday, the woman told Marcell she wanted money to fix up the house and also to buy a television and a radio. Marcell protested that he had spent too much already on the *bonoeman* and that he had other debts to pay as well as saving for her ticket to Holland. She then said that she wanted to have a baby with him. Marcell refused. In the first place, it would make it more difficult for her to go to Holland (she still did not want to go) and it would also foist more responsibility on him. If she got pregnant Marcell promised he would beat her. The woman does not use contraceptives, but years ago went to a Javanese masseuse. The Javanese undergo folk massage treatment which causes prolapsus of the uterous thus rendering them temporarily sterile. This is widely known in Suriname.

The next week found Marcell at home sitting quite domestically with the woman. The objects of their admiration were a new television and radio. He had taken out a loan at work and bought them that very day (the television for Sf 450 and the radio for Sf 50).

Before leaving for the *winkel*, he would cermoniously pour a bottle of perfume in the calabash while the woman stared wide-eyed. Over rum he told her he was considering not sending her away if she continued to behave so well.

Life proceeded as usual. One evening at the *winkel* he announced to the men that he was now ready to act against his brother. They offered him little sympathy. Let sleeping dogs lie, they agreed. He was insistent and left for the *bonoeman's*.

Asking how things were going, the *bonoeman* nodded smugly when he heard of the woman's behavior. Marcell pointed out that plans must be made to punish his brother. The *bonoeman* hesitated. Very thoughtfully he focused his eyes on Marcell and told him it was better to forget about the brother. Marcell then asked about the woman's sister; he still wanted to hurt her for her complicity. The *bonoeman* again replied in the negative. Better, he told Marcell, if you concentrate on keeping the woman at home. In effect he was telling Marcell to concentrate on the sure thing and forget about other matters.

The *bonoeman* is no fool. As a born psychologist and one privy to gossip, he guessed the woman would have eventually returned to her benefactor Marcell. However, it was beyond his power supernaturally and socially to guarantee the results of the two rituals Marcell now wanted. It was the *winkel* men who would perform this service for Marcell.

Later, Marcell stopped at the *winkel* for a drink and a lengthy discussion of the characteristics of women. Although speaking in general Marcell used himself as an example. He repeatedly cited a common refrain: "If you do not provide for a woman, she will take another man" (*Efoe joe pina wan oema, a go teki tra man*). In short, a man can buy a woman's allegiance like a commodity. A man can have relationships with other women but, if he provides for his woman, she under no circumstances may *waka-waka* with other men. He spent the rest of the evening convincing himself that he must provide handsomely for the support of the woman. A few days later a new expensive electric frying pan sat proudly on a gleaming refrigerator. (Loans were arranged through his workplace.)

Gaining confidence, Marcell devised a new plan. Gradually losing interest in his brother and his woman's sister he told his friends he wanted to perform an "experiment" with the woman. The next week he would send her to her sister's house in Nickerie (a district bordering Guyana) for a week. If the woman came back from so far away it would be final proof that the series of ritual worked.

Other things helped determine this decision. Ever since the beginning of the ceremonies Marcell had continued seeing his old girl friends and had made new contacts. With the Javanese living with him he had no place to take these women. The next week he could take a week off and, with his woman away, entertain the women who have been beseeching him. As Marcell put it, "The dog looks for bones all the time, but sometimes the bone looks for the dog" (*A la ten dagoe soekoe bonjo, ma' solesi bonjo soekoe dagoe*).

The first day of Marcell's week off opened gloriously. He was his old pleasant, witty and gregarious self again. A drink of rum, a coy remak to a passing beauty and a joke shared with the assembled crew. Yesterday the woman left for Nickerie. The *bonoeman* also stopped by to borrow Sf 10. Four of his seven nights were spent with different women.

When the Javanese returned home, there was no special ceremony or welcome to mark her reentry. She confirmed the efficacy of the ritual; and why not, she had everything to gain.

During her absence, however, something happened. While sitting in the *winkel* Marcell was approached by a young woman. It was another one of the brother's women, the very one Marcell wanted to capture through magic. Marcell immediately assumed that he had undergone such a powerful sequence of rituals that, by contagion, he had brought her here under his umbrella of influence. Marcell, it seemed, was the master of his universe.

Seeing that she was in an advanced state of pregnancy, he decided against immediate sexual intercourse. She continued to visit him almost every night at the *winkel* for the next two weeks. During the course of their conversations she told him of the harsh and horrible treatment she suffered at the hands of his brother; how she was pregnant with not a guilder of support from anyone and how she would like to be with a man as powerful as Marcell.

Two weeks later Marcell disclosed a charge sheet from a hospital. On it was a schedule of charges for matenity care. His brother's woman had informed Marcell of her lack of money for hospital fees. Marcell agreed to pay fourth class costs. This would extend his supernatural control over her and the child. The *winkel* men felt he was foolish for spending money on a woman who was the responsibility of another man. Marcell said it was his ritual responsibility. The pregnant girl was merely acting out a role magically designed.

Riding through town the next day Marcell pointed out he had had no further contact with the *bonoeman*. Only occasionally the *bonoeman* comes to borrow money.

On the way home Marcell yelled through the window to a woman who turned out to be the Javanese woman's sister. The conversation started with her cursing him mightily. She had heard of his designs. He was calm and in complete control of the situation and after her outburst proceeded to smooth her ruffled feathers. Could he come to visit her and talk things over. Elevating nose skyward and squinting at him out of the corners of her eyes she replied yes.

Since starting out on his adventure into the realm of magic three months ago, Marcell had accomplished every one of the tasks he had set for himself. The direction, thrust and content of these goals have been modified by many outsiders, the most influential being the *bonoeman*. Marcell had first wanted a charm (*tapoe*) to protect him from suspected black magic (*wisi*) directed by his brother. The *wasi skin* (body washing) was performed and Marcell was not victimized.

Marcell wanted his woman to return and, after a lengthy series of ceremonies culminating in the capture of her spirit, the woman returned. The *bonoeman* had pointed out that the effect of this ritual may only be temporary.

Marcell wanted sexual access to the brother's latest woman. This he received and, since the birth of her children, Marcell initiated a visiting relationship with her. Although a specific ritual was never performed, Marcell felt that the totality of magical power generated by preceding rituals broke his brother's control and forced this woman to seek him out.

Marcell wanted sexual access to the Javanese woman's sister as a form of revenge for the treatment he suffered at her hands. The ritual for this was never performed. Marcell never did establish an intimate relationship with her, but they are on speaking terms and there are no obvious problems between them.

Both Marcell and the neighborhood are happy everything has worked out so well. Social equilibrium has been reestablished.

Marcell's problems were all solved by neighborhood level institutions and behavior patterns. The *winkel* was instrumental in effecting what Marcell wanted. It was a forum which acted as a conservative, advising body when Marcell had rash or dangerous plans. Daily he would tell the regulars what had happened and what his plans were. Word spread through gossip and everyone involved with Marcell, either for him or against him, knew what he was doing. When he decided not to physically beat the woman for her wayward behavior, but to forgive her, take her back and provision her the word went out by *mofo radio* (mouth radio). Word of his interest in the brother's destitute woman (and Marcell was widely recognized as a handsome provider) followed the same networks.

Marcell did not rely on the police, the courts, the church or specialized organs of the government to solve his problems. Nor did he turn to his closest relative Sissy (FaSi) and Sadie her daughter. Many times they did not have the slightest idea of what he was up to. Like many others they were critical or exploitive of his extravagant behavior; and once Sadie had asked him if, since the woman was gone, she could have his refrigerator. Marcell's father was called upon for sanction. During the ritual process Marcell continued with his remittances to both these parties.

Other unattached women in the neighborhood were standing by to take advantage of any lucrative change of events in his situation. As word spread that the woman left him, a number of women sought Marcell out. He would later, in a better state of mind, make contact with them.

His work suffered, but not irreparably. During the most intense phase of the rituals he missed on the average of two days a week. The high level Dutch and American bosses would neither tolerate nor understand Marcell's dilemma. Fortunately there were foremen and workers who understood his problem and could make excuses for him.

The *bonoeman*, of course, was necessary to the whole process. In the functioning of the neighborhood which was thrown out of equilibrium by Marcell's problem, the magical ceremonies were a catalyst and, through their suggestive powers and symbolic sanction of proper behavior, primed everyone involved. People were influenced to behave as the magic dictated. But people do not live in a mysterious world of supernatural processes. They live in a very real world concerned with eating, clothing, other human beings and their status in the community. As they followed the magical dictates of the ceremonies they were all behaving as they must and should act in acceptable community forms. Nothing strange or abberant resulted from the magic, only the expected and the normal. Marcell, and the entire local community, were acting in normal fashion as the rituals reconstructed and reconstituted social processes gone temporarily awry. Normal ground rules for interaction had been restored.

The *bonoeman* knew this and would not commit himself to a ritual that called for something against the community grain. The rituals to force the woman to return were elementary. Given what he knew about Marcell, the brother and the woman, the *bonoeman* knew it was only proper and logical that she come back. The charm to protect Marcell was not a careless excursion. No harm would come as long as he felt secure and safe from his own thoughts and fears. If the brother were to shoot him, that act would fall in the realm of the secular, something not guaranteed by this *tapoe*. All the actors in the drama did what was expected of them.

The woman is still living with Marcell. Marcell is still visiting his old girl friends. Marcell has not yet bought her a ticket to go to Holland (he cannot because he voluntarily has spent all his money on items to keep her with him). Marcell is his old self. By the standards of the men who participate in the *winkel* subculture Marcell is a very normal man — with a large budget.

Marcell's rite of passage from his aunt's household to a new household with concubine was more difficult than most. The general pattern of extra-residential mating with a series of women, fissioning off from a consanguineal household and eventual establishment of a (temporary) neo-local relationship required magical assistance.

Marcell's dilemma had upset relationships that previously had been in equilibrium. Normal inter-ethnic communication (Creole-Javanese) was strained. Inter-consanguine relationships were altered by the establishment of new residential arrangements. New conjugal relationships were reactivated or created. There had taken place an extreme case of male competition caused by a violation of brotherhood and a form of female exchange or sharing unacceptable by Creole standards. The immediate parties concerned and the neighborhood as a system could not cope with these altered states of interaction. Things had to be brought back to normal.

A marginal was brought in to right the wrongs and reestablish preferred patterns. The *bonoeman's* first step in the ritual restoration of normalcy was to create a myth for his client; a supernatural diagnosis. The brother and the woman were bewitched and Marcell would shortly fall under these evil spells if he did not seek supernatural aid and protection. Magical symbols were used rather than the formal state organs of police, courts, churches and insane asylums.

The series of rituals were a success and Marcell was able to reestablish a satisfactory male-female relationship. The Javanese does in fact behave as his slave but the role, as he defines it, differs but little from normal housewoman roles. Actually his choice of a Javanese woman as dependent housewoman was, for Marcell, wise; Creole women are much more independent and exercise a good deal more extra-household movement. Nothing extraordinary resulted from the rituals. Throughout this entire process Marcell did not deactivate any of his links to other households; in fact he added more through his growing contacts with accessible women. During all of this he frequented the *winkel,* as a way station between households and a place to go to interact with neutral "others" and is now regularly found there between work and visits with his women — aunt, cousin, lovers and concubine. For Marcell, all is back to "normal" for the time being.[32]

Chapter five — Conclusion

The transition to adulthood for a lower-class Creole male is marked largely by his access to capital resources, his financial maturity. Securing some measure of this, he simultaneously loosens his ties with the household of origin and spends more time at the *winkel* with his fellows. The age there varies from early twenties to sixties, as does income, which ranges from scarcely Sf 175 per month to salaries soaring over Sf 400 per month. While regularly participating in their *winkel* passtimes the men form their many and strategic relationships with women and households. Conjugal unions usually stabilize in later years when it is in a man's interest to consolidate his time and resources around one particular household.

The regular members of the *winkel* group, those men who congregate with greater frequency and regularity than other customers, have two things in common. First, viewed over a time span and barring temporary and incidental misfortune, they are all financially solvent. Second, they have maintained residential and domestic links with members of their consanguineal families while engaging in a variety of simultaneous mating relationships with a number of women.

Freilich (1961: 966) seeks to portray these sexual pairings as "serial polygyny" in the fashion of an equilibrium-seeking system. He observes that: "The frequent changing of spouses, which could act as a factor of instability in the system, is balanced by lifelong membership in a matrifocal family." In short, although males and females establish multiple mating relationships, they always have a consanguineal anchor to which they can return.

This is indeed accurate. Males can activate kinship ties and thereby lay claim to certain services through particular consanguines. But we must not visualize the process too simply; that is, as a one-dimensional sequence of events with a male leaving one woman, returning to his consanguines, establishing a new extra-residential mating arrangement, leaving his consanguinal base and finally reestablishing a visiting or residential relationship again.

Observation over time would suggest that a male has simultaneous and, often times, enduring relationships with a number of women, regardless of his present residence. Simply because he has moved away from a woman and back to his consanguines does not mean he has permanently dissolved the relationship with her or with any of the other women he was visiting while he was living with her.

Households are linked by chains of kinship, friendship and exchange relationships. For individuals, their dyadic ties with other households are regularly altered with contacts becoming activated, deactivated or reactivated as necessary. Elaborate support networks are maintained with these women though on a different order or frequency and content.

In 1956 R. T. Smith introduced the term matrifocality to refer to the central features of lower-class West Indian households. At once, other students began locating "matrifocal families" in the Old World and New, each with its own distinctive set of attributes, style, structure, personnel, mating system and so forth. Were it not for R. T. Smith's powerful remarks on the status of males in the socio-economic occupational hierarchy it is likely that some students would have missed the point of dealing with other relevant factors set in the context of a developmental cycle. Specific households, in genealogical or physical contact or not, are articulated by networks of males who provide support and household maintenance. The men (as well as the women) manipulate conjugal, consanguineal and friendship dyads in their strivings with the consequences of their relationships extending far beyond the boundaries of any one or two households.

As males pass through the life cycle they build up an increasing repertoire of ex-mates and children. These are part of a usable reserve of personal resources that surround ego. Not all the relationships with these personnel are activated, and it is unlikely that they would ever be activated all the same time. The result resembles a "quasi-group" (Mayer, 1966): a group of people – consanguines, lovers, friends, *winkel* crew, etc. – that surrounds ego and provides him with a wide source of exploitable social capital. When ego strategically contacts certain persons that may have lain dormant in his quasi-group, he activates about him an "action set" that is cohesive (for ego) and exists for the duration of his needs. For a service, or series of different services, perhaps mutually exclusive but occuring at the same time, ego may draw upon different persons within his group to expedite his needs.

The men at the *winkel* talk constantly about being "good men" (*goede man* and *boen soema* in Dutch and *Sranan Tongo* respectively) and try regularly to maintain this image with their fellow cohorts. Should someone intentionally or unintentionally break this informal code by, for example, attempting to be something he is not (Russel's new radio), being expecially bellicose, or abusing the support mechanisms of the group, there are active status leveling devices that reestablish equilibrium. The men like to think that they are all equal, although it is obvious they are not and display it in their behavior. There is an ingroup status hierarchy. However, the intra-group differences should never be explicitly stated or thrown into sharp relief for this would upset and overwhelm the threads and themes that draw the men together.

The *winkel* is accessible to men. There are no strict entrance requirements, scheduled commitments or rites of passage. A well behaved man with a good reputation must merely drop by and make his presence known. At the beginning, the *winkel* group will be cautious, but after observing the stranger over a period of time, discussing his background and finding his qualities acceptable, the porous group boundaries absorb him. Departure is just as easy; one leaves. This type of behavior is replicated in a man's dealings with women. The nature of interaction between men and between men and women is quite similar. Other than agreeable conversation and financial solvency, the *winkel* places no stringent requirements on the crew members. Many keep erratic schedules and drop in when circumstances permit. However, they are redrawn into the group.

The relationships men form with women, as conjugals and consanguines, are subject to frequent disturbances: departures, prolonged recurrent or non-recurrent absences, shifting, multiple alliances erratically altering the flow of goods and services and so forth. The nature of sexual pairing, tolerating multiple relationships, can breed hostility and jealousy between men and women. For men, whose relationships span many households, the discharge of rights, responsibilities and obligations becomes confusing, conflicting and many times impossible to satisfy. Men are regularly placed in positions of potential discord and conflict between households often devolves upon them. Interaction between men and women can be erratic and irregular with the relationships themselves brittle, shifting and semi-permanent as men and women work and re-work their uses of time, space and personnel to adapt to immediate circumstances created by either the larger environment or individual choice.

In this potentially turbulent atmosphere the *winkel* can function as one means whereby men can mediate disturbance in their interaction. The *winkel,* in the sense that Chapple and Coon (1942) use the term, is their "association." In this social organization, this clockwork, more goes on at the *winkel* than merely the consumption of alcohol and lounging around. Social adjustments to changes in domestic and employment status are acted out symbolically and socially in the *winkel* and are signalled by changes in the structure and content of a man's network transactions. The *winkel* is their club, their forum. The men did not "flee here" nor are they "failures." Larger society downtown, more prosperous, more European, and, the other ethnic groups in Suriname, dot not understand the men and muse over their seeming idleness.

What I have described is a common pattern for lower-status Creole males in Paramaribo. Indeed, the behavior here is not unique. Wilson (1974) has taken us on a "Caribbean Cruise" to Jamaica, Barbados, Guyana, Trinidad, Carriacou, the Andros Islands and Belize to compare similar data from these areas with his own findings on the structure and sentiment of male peer groups ("crews") in Providencia. The behaviors demonstrated in these places, along with the material from Paramaribo, suggest tremendous regional similarity at certain socio-economic levels — as was once the investigative point of departure for studies of the "matrifocal" family. Object and sample in time and space were extremely important here. To grasp the nature of an adult man as a broker linking households, and with various modes of participation spanning many households, I had to go beyond "household" itself as focus. The *winkel* as social and spatial focus of much male interaction seemed to minimally satisfy this requirement.

One more aspect of Paramaribo Creole male social organization remains to be considered. The huge body of literature on the Afro-American family suggests, sometimes tacitly, sometimes explicitly, that for poorer Black males "home" is a place where his "inadequacies" are thrown into sharp relief and where he is often assailed with humiliation and ridicule by groups of related "women" (themselves in desperate economic straits). However, these tensions, in whatever form they may exist, do not adaquately explain why, for Paramaribo Creoles at any rate, men spend so much of their time "on the streets" and in "public" areas. If one assumes they should be other places, doing other things, at other times, with other people the slip to a mildly deviant interpretation of their behavior is an easy one to make. Misguided propriety may suggest that when not "working" (9 to 5 one is led to presume) a man should be in the company of his "family" or when not spending leisure time with family one should be at work. Insinuated also, is that "acceptable" leisure time activities with male peer groups should be scheduled or routinized, on the order of Thursday night poker playing, or bowling, or drinking bouts, or whatever. The fellows in the *winkel* are then victimized by one or another perspective. Either they are shiftless, lazy and irresponsible ne'er do wells or they have, because of unhappy and blatantly exploitative historical circumstances, developed means of "adaptation" that do not "function" in their (and others') long term interests.

Caribbean, and Surinamese, history has been oppressive and the majority of

Conclusion

West Indians are victimized by institutions and sets of relationships that crystallized long ago. Given the organization of the society in which they live I said earlier that the men "may have no place else to go" than the *winkel*. But, the activities that go on in the *winkel* are brought about by individual men sharing their experiences in a forum they create, imbue with texture and charge with meaning. Though social circumstances may have directed them towards the *winkel* and set off this social and geographical place as "for lower-class Creole men" it is they themselves who make the experience worth tasting, create situations in which they choose to participate and look forward everyday to exercise their choice and return there. If the *winkel* is one of their "alternatives" in Surinamese social organization, they certainly make the most of it and it is a pleasure for them.

These men have adapted to their circumstances and they are quite as aware as anybody else that their *winkel*-world is not a self-contained, self-generating system or sub-system with clear boundaries. The streetcorner behavior demonstrated by these men is in large part a response to a system that demands little else from them. Given their circumstances, the mating system, household organization and the men's status in the occupational hierarchy — all relationships characterized by loose, shifting and irregular interaction — these men need the compensation that their shop sanctuary provides. Besides, the men enjoy the drinking, camaraderie, ballyhoo and story-telling, and that is reason enough to go "on the corner".

Appendix

The narrative is an outgrowth of my doctoral dissertation research (University of Florida, 1974). A total of 22 months (February, 1972 to December, 1973) were spent in Paramaribo and certain of its rural environs. I will conclude with some fairly standard fieldwork remarks.

Apart from participant-observation encounters data were also retrieved from newspapers, independent publications, radio and television, government and private offices, formal interviews with civil servants and policy makers and reference to the archives. Approximately seventy-five percent of the research time was spent in Paramaribo, while the remainder was devoted to two rural Creole districts.

The study involved the learning of two languages. The city dialect of *Sranan Tongo,* a creole language with an identifiably English grammer and English, Dutch, French, Portuguese and African derivitives in the lexicon was the main research tool. Except when speaking with the formally educated and upper classes (though there were exceptions) all verbal information retrieval was in this language. We chose this language, as opposed to the official Dutch, because it presented a Creole perception of the environment they inhabit complete with sanctions, shades of meaning and feelings that one would be unable to comprehend in the "school learned" language.

The Dutch language was a passive research tool and we used it for reading and listening. Virtually all written material for Creole consumption in Suriname, aside from a growing body of poetry, is in Dutch. Radio broadcasts vary; and in the course of one day in Paramaribo one could hear the following languages on radio channels: Dutch, Hindi, Urdu, Sranan Tongo, "Javanese," Chinese, two Bush Negro languages, English and French.

Television is almost entirely in Dutch except for "cultural" programming and North American movies and serials. The languages used in public meetings, addresses and forums varies with the situation and the audience. Multi-ethnic gatherings were usually addressed in Dutch so as to show no linguistic bias or favoritism of any one group.

Three months after our arrival and with enough Sranan Tongo under our belts to make us intelligible, we moved to a neighborhood and into a house that would neither scandalize upper-status visitors with its shabbiness nor deter lower-status persons from dropping by with its opulence.

It is necessary here to bring in some personal information. I have always been interested in male behavior, whether in the context of drinking, fighting, gambling, cavorting, fraternizing, householding or working. I have tried to look at these behavioral sets in their totality rather than as discrete types of activities. However, I have always been limited by the fact that I could never, with a great deal of accuracy, get good comparative, genuine, open information from women. This circumstance varies from society to society. Although in Suriname a male anthropologist can approach a female Creole and get reasonably frank information, there are limitations.

Upon our arrival Rosemary Brana-Shute and I continually collaborated on refining research design and ethnographic retrieval. I spent nearly all my time with males in male associated activities; she did the same with women. We like to think that we overcame many of the biases and misunderstandings built into a situation where the sex of the researcher permits a close, and perhaps self-fulfilling, association with one group and perhaps little more than a stereotyped relationship with the other.

After our separate day's work we would gather together our data and discuss what I heard and how I heard it with what she had. Each day we would try and explore similar topics. The different accounts were illuminating. One example should make this clear.

One day there was a fight between a man and a woman in the neighborhood. Reportedly, she went after him with a machete threatening to cut off his head. At the time of the eruption I was sitting with my friends in the *winkel* while Rosemary was in a neighboring back yard visiting friends. When the fight broke out the men descended upon the street and ran up the block to witness the fermentation. At the same time the women poured out onto the street. In the ensuing shuffle the women took away the weapons and hid them, pulled the female antagonist away and left the male standing with his fellows. They then spirited her away to the back yard while we retreated to the *winkel*. What happened at my end was a long tale of woe condemning women and decrying their mean characteristics. Commentary was offered by the attendant commiserators. Long accounts of prior indignities followed; and, related with great detail, they cited time, place, circumstance and personnel. The ethnographer was listening attentively. Rosemary, on the other hand, was in the thick of it with the women who held forth in the same tenor as the men. Stories flew, especially about economic, familial and personel male irresponsibility.

What resulted was a marvelous complementary picture of what happened and how the different sexes felt about it. Had only I been there, I would have heard the tale in great and gory detail from the men and gathered only a superficial version from the women. We combined, compared and contrasted data all during the research period.

Most of my time was spent with a group of men who congregated more or less regularly in a street corner *winkel* in the research area. With some men there was warm mutual respect and admiration, with others there was casual indifference and with some there was genuine dislike.

All data collected were correlated with information garnered in other segments of the neighborhood and Paramaribo, in *winkels*, households, at dances, at work places and through interviews with those in positions of power and authority.

Future work will deal with the cultural context of juvenile delinquency.

Notes

1. See Lowenthal, 1972; Lewis, 1968; and Hoetink, 1967 for a general regional introduction to the nature of color, class and cultural perception in the Caribbean.
2. Michelle Z. Rosaldo's "Woman, Culture and Society: A Theoretical Overview," in Rosaldo and Lamphere (1974: 17-42), is a critical statement on some of the flaws inherent in "matrifocal thinking." In effect, where sex roles are presumed to be strictly divided between the domestic and public spheres, a negative valance will be placed on woman's activities. This sexual asymmetry may "lead us to ignore the manifold ways in which women in different social systems achieve power and a sense of personal value" (Rosaldo and Lamphere 1974: 9).
3. An explanation of my continued reference to "Creole" as well as Suriname's membership in the Caribbean cultural community is included in the Foreward.
4. Until 1975 Suriname was an "Autonomous member of the Kingdom of the Netherlands." The country obtained its independence on November 25, 1975 and is now officially known as the Republic of Suriname. The only complete social history of Suriname is still that of van Lier, 1971. This publication is the English translation of a 1949 volume and includes an appended chapter in the year of republication.
5. Sranan Tongo ("Suriname Language"), an English based creole language, is the traditional language of Creole Surinamers and is spoken widely by the lower-classes and rural residents. See Voorhoeve and Lichtveld, 1975.
6. It would be instructive to read Mintz's discussion of "Houses and Yards among Caribbean Pesantries." (Mintz, 1974).
7. This is a very rough estimate calculated by using the population of voting districts that overlap and comprise part(s) of *Frimangron*. There is no census of the neighborhood.
8. "Liming" is the English-speaking Creole term widely used in the Caribbean to mean "hanging-out" or standing on the street or corner with no ostensible purposes other than the one apparent. One seems to have nothing to do and to be doing nothing. In fact, however, one may be "doing" a great deal.
9. At the time (1971-1974) the value of one Suriname Florin (Sf) was 57 U.S. dollar cents.
10. Russel's salary is typical of that for unskilled laborers. According to government officials in Paramaribo the "unofficial" minimum wage is Sf 250 per month for a man, woman and four children. As will be pointed out, few lower-status men in Paramaribo live in a permanent fixed arrangement with a woman and children, and, rarely, is one monthly salary for the exclusive use of one household.

11 Marcell makes one of the highest salaries in the neighborhood and were it not for his entangling relationships and *winkel* expenditures could easily amass a sizable sum of money. He has, however, elaborated on the lower-class pattern and instead of supporting a few women on a small salary supports a number of women on a large salary.
12 This point was brought rather sharply home when the ethnographer, one accustomed to storing money in banks, desperately needed 50 guilders one Sunday afternoon. Thanks to my friend I got it.
13 During my graduate preparation for field work and during the early stages of the research itself, I was regularly tempted to refer to such streetcorner congeries of males with Peter Wilson's term "crews" (1973). However, Wilson's Providencia crews are more tightly knit, homogeneous and enduring than the group(s) of men I describe. Also, the Paramaribo men do not explicitly see themselves as a "crew" nor do they act like it.
14 Political competition between Creoles and Hindustani (East Indians), the two largest ethnic groups in Suriname, was keen and when one of the groups achieved government control waves of patronage would follow for their supporters. See van Lier, 1971 and Kruijer, 1973. Since Independence there have emerged coalition parties cutting across ethnic boundaries and a guarded commitment to integration and solidarity.
15 In my early stages of observation in the *winkel* I intuitively felt that there was something special about the 15 or so men and that they felt something special about each other. In an attempt to dignify my feelings I wrote down the names of the men on seperate index cards as well as the names of other known boys and men inside and outside of the neighborhood. I had a total of about 40 cards. In private I then individually asked each of the 15 men to "sort out the cards into piles" in any categories they wished and to give me the reasons for their choices. Though there was some variation, based more on my confused directions than anything else, the 15 names of the *winkel* "men" usually came up in the same pile. When asked why such a distribution was made, the men gave "he's trustworthy and does not gossip," "he's not a mooch," etc., all qualities that would also account for the inclusion of outsiders. None of the 15 respondents said "because he is with our *winkel* crew." After some time as a guest of the *winkel* I came to appreciate these qualities in the men. This attempt to plumb the cognitive categories of the men was taught to me by Dr. Michael Kenny of Catholic University who supervised a summer field school in Northern Idaho in 1970 in which I had the privilege to participate.
16 To be a good talker, of course, is also a culture trait that crosses ethnic and class lines. Thus speech making and toast-making are still studied arts in Suriname and the man who is a good "speaker" usually gathers a substantial following; the political arena providing us with perhaps the best example.
17 This appreciation of personal qualities has been described by Wilson (1973) for the contemporary Caribbean and he suggests that the opposition between streetcorner "reputation" and the manners and morals of "respectable" society are a polar ambiguity. The two sit as: " . . . a precariously tensile structure of relationships between antithetical systems. On the one hand there is the imposed, alien structure of domination premised on inequality and stratification, while facing it is the autocthonous structure premised on differentiation and equality . . ." (219).
18 Mintz and Price (1976), in a sensitive discussion of the development of Afro-American culture, point to the traditional framework in which elaboration of personal qualities and attributes is appreciated: "Within the strict limits set by the conditions of slavery, Afro-Americans learned to put a premium on innovation and individual creativity; there was always a place for fads and fashion; "something new" (within certain aesthetic limits, of course) became something to be

celebrated, copied and elaborated ... (26). And: "Early on, then, the slaves were elaborating upon ways in which they could be individuals — a particular sense of humor, a certain skill or type of knowledge, even a distinctive way of walking or talking, or some sartorial detail, like the cock of a hat or the use of a cane" (26).

19 For an interesting discussion of middle and upper-class black clubs, see Manning, 1973. These groupings are quite different in symbol and structure from those of the *winkel* men.
20 For discussions of the time dimension in inter-action theory see Arensberg and Kimball, 1965; Chapple and Coon, 1942; Homans, 1950; and Boissevain, 1974.
21 Fox states (1967: 167): "... ego's cognates up to a certain degree are recognized as having some duties towards him and some claims on him. It is perhaps wrong to call this a 'group' at all, but rather we should call it a category of persons. It is never a residential unit nor is it corporate, and it only comes to life when the purpose for which it exists arises ..."
22 Buschkens (1974) encountered this among his sample of lower-class Creoles in Paramaribo. On page 152 he offers the following statement and chart: "Households with female heads receive a good deal of income from non-household members." This occurred in 78 of his 224 samples of all household types. The following chart outlines the nature of his finds:

Person Outside Household	Household with Male Head (n = 294)	Household with Female Head (n = 224)
Spouse	x	6
Friend	x	12
ex-Spouse	x	7
Son	6	28
Daughter	x	5
Other	9	20

23 Every fifth birthday following the twenty-fifth birthday takes on a more spiritual air. The person is approaching eldership (*bigi soema* — sixty and older) and as such is privy to all knowledge and status that old age brings. For people forty and older birthday party music (*bigi pokoe*) frequently turns into spirit cult music (*winti*) during the later hours of the celebration. The celebrant and some attendants are usually possessed by their *winti*.

On a purely sociological level, fifth year celebrations (*bigi jari*) in later years draw together huge crowds of kin, friends and neighbors for dancing, singing, eating, drinking, gossiping and possible communion with the spirit world.

24 See Wooding (1972) for a discussion of rural *winti* cults function in the context of overlapping and propinquitous cognatic descent groups.
25 This is not meant to sound like pious or soggy social work. I am aware that nuclear family, middle class monogomous unions are plagued by problems as well. I suggest here that the nature and degree of the "problems" encountered justify my statement. Also, I am not using "problem" in an abstract, academic, methodological sense. The men and women themselves use the word regularly and refer to the whole situation as *"moelijkheid"* (difficulty).
26 In discussing Marcell's relationship with this woman, I do not call her by her name, but rather refer to her as the "Javanese," "the woman," or the "Javanese woman." I am recounting the story through Creole eyes and never once did Marcell, the *winkel* men, nor the neighborhood women call the woman by her name (nor did they care to learn it). When on good terms with the woman

Marcell would occasionally refer to her as "my child" (*mi pikin*). The woman was a non-person to the Creoles except on two ritual occasions. This is explained in the text.
27 For a discussion see van Lier, 1971.
28 See Herskovits, 1936 for some interesting examples of Creole manners, morales and ethics.
29 See Price, 1976 for a discussion of the different Bush Negro tribes of Suriname.
30 Bush Negro magical practicioners are considered more powerful and skillful in manipulating the supernatural than Creole practicioners. Although most Creoles attend Creole *bonoeman* for their services, the "deeper" magic is the province of Bush Negroes. However, there is a dilemma here. Since the Bush Negroes are so powerful, and widely considered to be mysterious and sometimes barbaric, there is an element of potential danger in becoming their client. Deprecating stereotypes are widely foisted on Bush Negroes by urban Creoles.
31 There are more complicated catagories of magical practicioners in Creole eyes. The catagories overlap and depending on the situation or rite to be performed a practicioner may be a *loekoeman* (diviner or diagnostician), a *bonoeman* (practioner of theraputic magic) or a *wisiman* (practioner of black magic). Some magicians do only *bonoe* (theraputic) while others do all types. The man Marcell knows calls himself a *bonoeman* and never has been referred to differently though it is known he does *wisi* (sorcery). For a more complete discussion of this see Wooding, 1972.
32 Marcell's case is at the same time common and unique for lower-class men. The problems that had befallen him and, indeed, those that he created for himself through a mismanaged love and domestic life, occur regularly to lower-class men.

The mating relationships of most of these men are characterized by regular, short term disturbances which soon settle into an ongoing equilibrium. Marcell's case is intense, and was characterized by such a degree of disequilibrium the relationships involved could not be brought back into harmony by normal means. In great part this was due to Marcell's seemingly masochistic behavior and personality. The dilemma itself, however, was not unique.

Bibliography

Algemeen Bureau voor de Statistiek
1973 Voorlopig Resultaat Vierde Algemene Volkstelling.
    Suriname in Cijfers, No. 60. Paramaribo.
Arensberg, Conrad M. and Solon T. Kimball
1965 Culture and Community. New York: Harcourt, Brace and World Inc.
Beckford, George
1972 Persistent Poverty. New York: Oxford
Bender, D. R.
1967 A refinement of the Concept of Household: Families, Coresidence and Domestic Function. *American Anthropologist* 69: 493-504.
Blau, Peter
1964 Exchange and Power in Social Life. New York: John Wiley and Sons.
Boissevain, Jeremy
1974 Friends of Friends: Networks, Manipulators and Coalitions. Oxford: Basil, Blackwell.
Boissevain, Jeremy and J. C. Mitchell (eds)
1973 Network Analysis Studies in Human Interaction. The Hague: Mouton.
Bovenkerk, Frank
1976 Wie Gaat er Terug naar Suriname: Een Onderzoek naar de Retourmigratie 1972-1973. Amsterdam: Anthropological-Sociological Center, University of Amsterdam.
Brana-Shute, Gary
1974 Streetcorner *Winkels* and Dispersed Households: Male Adaptation to Marginality in a Lower-Class Creole Neighborhood in Paramaribo. Doctoral Dissertation. University of Florida.
1976 Drinking Shops and Social Structure: Some Ideas on Lower-Class Male West Indian Behavior. *Urban Anthropology*, Vol. 5, No. 1.
1978 Some Aspects of Youthful Identity Management in a Paramaribo Creole Neighborhood. *De Nieuwe West Indische Gids*, Vol. 53, No. 1.
Brana-Shute, Rosemary
1976 Women, Clubs and Politics: The Case of a Lower-Class Neighborhood in Paramaribo. *Urban Anthropology*, Vol. 5, No. 2.
Brana-Shute, R. and G. Brana-Shute
1977 A Death in the Family: Mourning Rituals in a Creole Community. Mededelingen of the Suriname Museum, Monograph Series, No. 21.

Bruijne, G. A. de
1976 Paramaribo, Stadsgeografische studies van een ontwikkelingsland. Bussum: Roman.
Buschkens, W. F. L.
1974 The Family System of the Paramaribo Creoles.
 The Hague: Martinus Nijhoff.
Centraal Bureau Luchtkartering
1965 Map of Area within Paramaribo. Blad 144 C and D. Scale 1:1000. Paramaribo.
Chapple, Eliot and Carlton Coon
1942 Principles of Anthropology. New York: Henry Holt.
Clarke, Edith
1957 My Mother Who Fathered Me. London: Ruskin House,Ltd.
Demas, William G.
1965 The Economics of Development in Small Countries with Special Reference to the Caribbean. Montreal: McGill University Press.
de Waal Malefijt, Annemarie
1963 The Javanese of Surinam. Assen: van Gorcum and Co.
Douglas, Mary
1966 Purity and Danger. New York: Prager.
Foster, George
1961 The Dyadic Contact: A Model for the Social Structure of a Mexican Village. *American Anthropologist* 63: 1173-1192.
Fox, Richard
1977 Urban Anthropology: Cities in their Cultural Setting. Englewood Cliffs, N.J.: Prentice Hall.
Frazier, E. Franklin
1939 The Negro Family in the United States. Chicago: University Press.
Freilich, Morris
1961 Serial Polygyny, Negro Peasants, and Model Analysis. *American Anthropologist* 63: 955-975.
Gans, Herbert J.
1962 The Urban Villagers. Glencoe: The Free Press.
Glaser, Barney and Anselm Strauss
1967 The Discovery of Grounded Theory. Chicago: Aldine.
Goffman, Erving
1959 The Presentation of Self in Everyday Life. New York: Doubleday.
Gonzalez, Nancie L.
1970 Toward a Definition of Matrifocality. In Afro-American Anthropology: Contemporary Perspectives. Norman E. Whitten and John F. Szwed, eds. New York: Free Press.
Greenfield, Sidney
1966 English Rustics in Black Skin. New Haven: College Press.
Henriques, F. M.
1953 Family and Color in Jamaica. London: Eyre and Spottiswoode.
Herskovits, Melville J.
1937 Life in a Haitian Valley. New York: Knopf.
Herskovits, Melville J. and Francis S. Herskovits
1936 Suriname Folklore. Columbia University Contributions to Anthropology, 27. New York: Columbia University Press.
Hoetink, H.
1967 Caribbean Race Relations: A Study of Two Variants. London: Oxford University Press.

Homans, George
1950 The Human Group. New York: Harcourt, Brace and World.
Hooghart, D. A.
1973 Demografische Structuur van Ons Volk. In 100 Jaar Suriname: Gedenkboek i.v.m. Een Eeuw Immigratie (1873-1973). J. H. Adhin, ed. Paramaribo: Stichting Hindoestaanse Immigratie.
Kloos, Peter
1971 The Maroni River Caribs of Surinam. Assen: van Gorcum.
Kruijer, G. J.
1973 Suriname: Neokolonie in Rijksverband. Meppel: Boom.
Lamur, H. E.
1973 The Demographic Evolution of Surinam, 1920-1970.
The Hague: Martinus Nijhoff.
Lewis, Gordon
1968 The Growth of the Modern West Indies. New York: Modern Reader Paperbacks.
Liebow, Eliot
1967 Tally's Corner. Boston: Little Brown.
Lofland, John
1971 Analyzing Social Settings. Belmont: Wadsworth.
Lowenthal, David
1972 West Indian Societies. New York: Oxford University Press.
Manning, Frank E.
1973 Black Clubs in Bermuda. Ithaca: Cornell University.
Matza, David
1969 Becoming Deviant. Englewood Cliffs, N.J.: Prentice Hall.
Mayer, Adrian
1966 The Significance of Quasi-Groups in the Study of Complex Societies. A.S.A. Monograph 4. Michael Banton, ed. London: Travistock.
Mintz, Sidney
1974 Caribbean Transformations, Chicago; Aldine Publishing Co.
1966 The Caribbean as Socio-Cultural Area. *Cahiers d'Histoire Mondiale* IX: 916-41.
Mintz, Sidney and Richard Price
1976 An Anthropological Approach to the Afro-American Past: A Caribbean Perspective. Occasional Papers in Social Change, 2. Philadelphia: Institute for the Study of Human Issues.
Mitchell, J. C. (ed)
1969 Social Networks and Urban Situations. Manchester: University Press.
Mumford, Lewis
1938 The Culture of Cities. New York: Harcourt, Brace and World.
Naipaul, V. S.
1962 The Middle Passage. Middlesex: Penguin Books.
Noble, Mary
1973 Social Network: Its Use as a Conceptual Framework in Family Analysis. In Boissevain and Mitchell (eds.), Network Analysis Studies in Human Interaction. The Hague: Mouton.
Pierce, B. E.
1970 Kinship and Residence Among the Urban *Nengre* of Suriname. Doctoral Dissertation: Tulane University.
Price, Richard

1976 The Guiana Maroons: A Historical and Bibliographical Introduction. Baltimore: Johns Hopkins.

Radcliffe-Brown, A. R. and Daryll Forde, (eds).
1950 African Systems of Kinship and Marriage. London: Oxford University.

Rosaldo, Michelle Z. and Louise Lamphere (eds)
1974 Woman, Culture and Society. Stanford: University Press.

Smith, M. G.
1962 West Indian Family Structure. Seattle: University of Washington.

Smith, R. T.
1956 The Negro Family in British Guiana. London: Routledge and Kegan Paul Ltd.
1963 Culture and Social Structure in the Caribbean. *Comparative Studies in Society and History* 6: 24-45.

Solien Gonzalez, Nancie L.
1969 Black Carib Household Structure. Seattle: University of Washington.

Speckmann, J. D.
1965 Marriage and Kinship among the Indians in Surinam. Assen: van Gorcum.

Steward, Julian *et al.*
1956 People of Puerto Rico. Urbana: University of Illinois.

The Twinklestars
1974 The Twinklestars (Long Playing record album). Paramaribo.

VACO
n.d. Kaart van Paramaribo. Paramaribo: Kersten and Co.

Valentine, Charles A.
1968 Culture and Poverty. Chicago: University of Chicago Press.

van Lier, R. A. J.
1971 Frontier Society: A Social Analysis of the History of Surinam. The Hague: Martinus Nijhoff.

Volders, J. L.
1966 Bouwkunst in Suriname. Hilversum: G. van Saane.

Voorhoeve, Jan and Ursy M. Lichtveld
1975 Creole Drum: An Anthology of Creole Literature in Surinam. New Haven: Yale University Press.

Wagley, Charles
1957 Plantation America: A Cultural Sphere. Caribbean Studies: A Symposium. Seattle: University of Washington Press.

Whitten, Norman
1965 Class, Kinship and Power in an Equadorian Town. Stanford: University Press.

Williams, Eric
1970 From Columbus to Castro: The History of the Caribbean, !492-1969. New York: Harper and Row.

Wilson, Peter
1973 Crab Antics: The Social Anthropology of English-Speaking Negro Societies of the Caribbean. New Haven: Yale University Press.
1971 Caribbean Crews: Peer Groups and Male Society.
   Caribbean Studies, Vol. 10, No. 4.

Wooding, Charles
1972 Winti: Een Afro-Amerikaanse Godsdienst in Suriname.
   Meppel: Krips Repro. B.V.